Mother's Day Miracle

The Rita Chretien Story

Survival in the Nevada Wilderness

Rita Harter

ISBN 978-1-0980-2122-1 (paperback)
ISBN 978-1-0980-2124-5 (hardcover)
ISBN 978-1-0980-2123-8 (digital)

Copyright © 2020 by Rita Harter

All rights reserved. No part of this publication may be reproduced, distributed, or transmitted in any form or by any means, including photocopying, recording, or other electronic or mechanical methods without the prior written permission of the publisher. For permission requests, solicit the publisher via the address below.

Christian Faith Publishing, Inc.
832 Park Avenue
Meadville, PA 16335
www.christianfaithpublishing.com

Printed in the United States of America

CONTENTS

Acknowledgements...5
Introduction...7
1. Leaving for Las Vegas 9
2. Stranded and Alone...15
3. The Terrible Parting 23
4. Ice Hearts to Feathered Friend..27
5. Survival Mode 31
6. Bone-Chilling Battles 35
7. Thoughts of Home..41
8. Overcoming Fear...47
9. Forty Days 53
10. Hearing My Voice 56
11. Homeward Bound...59
12. The Great Rescue 63
13. The Royal Treatment 68
14. Home Sweet Home 77
15. Sweet Memories 83
16. Rita's New Normal 87
17. Tour of Gratitude 92
18. Closure at Last 97
19. Family History 103
20. As Long as We Both Shall Live.....................................107
21. Life with Albert...113
22. Albert's Memorial 117
23. Life after Death 122

ACKNOWLEDGEMENTS

I would like to say a big thank you to Theresa McRae White, who did many hours of research and interviews with family and friends. Theresa was a huge encouragement to me to get my story ready to share. I could not have done it without her inspiration to get it to completion.

Words cannot express my gratitude to the rescue teams and the many volunteers who searched for us relentlessly. My sincere thanks and appreciation to friends and family, many of who went out to search the highways. You and thousands of caring people prayed earnestly for my husband Albert and I to be found. God bless you all!

I thank my sons for believing in miracles and for not giving up. I am very proud of them for keeping well and for rallying together as a family. They were very responsible in the way they took care of our family business and our personal matters while we were missing and after many weeks assumed that we had perished.

I thank our faithful employees who stuck with my family and did everything possible to support them in that stressful time. Together they were strong.

My community rallied around my family when all hope was running thin! Neighbours and friends helped out beyond the call of duty. My church family didn't stop praying for a miracle! God answered prayer, not exactly as we had hoped, but His plans are higher than our plans.

INTRODUCTION

My life has not been the same since I returned home from Nevada. I can truly say that I have been enriched through my unplanned sabbatical from my comfortable life at home. My daily conscious decision to lean on *God Power,* not my own, built my inner strength for each day when each moment of fear swept over me like a wave.

Today, life is not perfect and easy but I am stronger and able to face the challenges with confidence. I am truly blessed and enjoy my life to the fullest, realizing it is very much my responsibility to make the best of my circumstances. An attitude of gratitude has saturated my heart and life, only possible because of faith in Jesus Christ my Saviour, who made my life worth living. My wilderness experience has been a great teacher to my soul. I am still a student and will be until the day I go to my eternal home.

I have come to realize that I need to share my story about my forty-nine-day wilderness experience in the spring of 2011. I would like to share with family, friends and others, so they can have a glimpse of what I went through and hopefully gain hope and inspiration in their own lives in whatever circumstances they are going through, now or from the past. Pain and suffering, whether physical, emotional, or spiritual, is not pleasant at any time but it can be a tremendous growth experience. Being transparent is scary and it would be easier to pretend it did not happen, but not sharing my experience would be like hiding my treasure in a deep hole never to be seen again.

I am thankful to God for the extended time he has given to me to live life well with more years to enjoy family and friends and more recently to share life's joys with my new husband, Dale.

I dedicate my writings to my late husband, Albert Chretien. May God be honoured!

Rita Harter

Chapter One

Leaving for Las Vegas

CONEXPO 2011 was set to feature 2,400 construction industry exhibitors and attract 125,000 delegates, from 150 countries. Billed as the largest global industry gathering place in North America for construction trade and material industries, it promised an "immense unveiling" of the latest and greatest equipment, technology, groundbreaking innovations and product breakthroughs.

Through the winter of 2011, Al's excitement kept on growing. At last, he was going to the construction industry's world mega-event in Las Vegas, Nevada. He had talked about this awesome trade show for several months. For my excavation expert husband, that was as big a deal as they get. Every three years CONEXPO came around, and each time, Al lobbied me to join him. No way in the world would Al go without me! As the years came and went, I let him dream on but my strategy was to let the clock run out until registration deadlines passed. This time was different. He was as determined and immovable as a boulder and I had run out of excuses. With frost still in the ground, March was normally a slower time for our family-owned excavating company, plus we had a capable crew that could handle the spring start-up.

Finally, I stopped dragging my heels. I agreed to go but on one condition: he had to promise he wouldn't purchase more equipment.

We took good care of all our company vehicles and machines and had all we needed. He assured me this trip was not for buying but "just for fun." I knew that would not hold water. He would think of a reason we needed a new excavator.

Personally, I could think of better definitions of fun than an equipment trade show. I would bring some books to read. It was always adventurous to travel with Al. We laid the groundwork to get away right after mid-March and return home before month-end to do payroll on time.

For Al, this trip would be a pre-retirement gift to himself, as well as a needed break from the hectic pace he kept. For me, it was a belated Valentine's date and a delayed celebration of our thirty-eighth anniversary. I also intended to take full advantage of the road time. With Al as a captive audience, we could pin down plans for our cross-Canada road trip for our future fortieth wedding anniversary in 2013.

Al counted the sleeps, like a kid looking forward to Christmas. On one of those countdown days, we joined in on a friend's ninetieth birthday celebration. There was an almost uncanny dreamlike quality to that gathering. Al was in his element, an irrepressible extrovert in the epicenter of the laughter and fun. At a quieter moment as we sat side-by-side on a loveseat, a friend asked us to pose for a photo. We smiled at the camera, as we turned to smile at each other. Al's eyes reflected a depth of love for me that was even deeper than on our honeymoon. His face was radiant. In admiration of him, I thought to myself, "He looks ready for heaven." As it turned out, millions of people world-wide had the opportunity to see that picture before I ever did.

The day before our departure day, we stopped by our eldest son's to give Deklan, our grandson, his sixth birthday gift, a truck and horse trailer. We gave big hugs all around. We'd see them again at the end of March. I packed light for sunny Nevada: a couple of dressy outfits, shoes, and a pair of dress boots, jeans, and a pair of light runners. For the trade show, Al packed his warmish Mack Tools jacket, his work boots, blue jeans and shirts, casual shoes, a dress shirt, and pants. We wore our spring jackets and took along a couple of warmer light-weight jackets for a cooler day. We always had a few wool toques and gloves, branded with our company logo, stashed away under the seat of our van. Anything more we needed we could always pick up along the way. Even though I really did not want to go I decided in advance that I was not going to fret over anything at all on this trip. I was going to enjoy every single minute of our lovely free time. I had to get on my knees and pray about this because I had fear after a scary nightmare about going away from home so far! I felt the Lord was telling me to be a good wife, be a good sport, support my husband and share in his joy!

Then the departure day came. It was March 19, 2011. The sun rose on a picture-perfect note. Little did we know our lives would be changed forever! Aiming for an early departure, Al had us in our brown 2000 Chevy Astro van at precisely 6:00 a.m. Before even leaving the driveway, I felt a hesitation and told him, "I think I forgot some things." He patiently watched morning rays filter over the hills while I rushed back in the house to finish scurry-packing last-minute items. In the kitchen, I spied an empty ice cream bucket and decided to take along my vitamins. Out of the corner of my eye, I caught sight of a full bottle of fish oil capsules and other vitamins that I did not have time to count enough for one week. I quickly popped them into the bucket. I grabbed four more small water bottles to add to the two I already had in our snack bag in the van. The snacks included a box of Triscuit crackers, a small zip lock bag of Trail Mix Nuts, a small zip lock bag of chocolate-covered Almonds, and another small bag of hard candies. The only other drinks we packed were four cans of soda pop.

As I was about to head out the door I had a memory flashback. I remembered the rainy, uncomfortable cool night when we had to sleep in the van at a highway truck stop when we couldn't find a vacant motel room. I never wanted to repeat that experience. I gathered up in my arms a few extra things at hand, two small wool quilts, and for good measure, a couple of travel pillows. Then I was out the door. I tossed the latest acquisitions onto the back seats and jumped into the front, set to go. I smiled at Al's expected response. "Why did you bring more stuff? We can always pick up more on the way.

And what's with the extra blankets and pillows? We won't need them. We're staying at motels." "Never you mind"—I shushed him—"better to have more than not enough! And you never know if we may want to stop for a nap."

Primed for adventure, we left our home behind and headed due south on Highway 97 toward the Canada-US border. Our spirits rose even higher with the rising sun. What lovely scenery along the way! Spring was in the air. Could life get any better than this? We had about twenty hours of driving ahead of us, two long days on the road. Penticton to Las Vegas is 1,970 kilometers (1,224 miles). Our return trip plan was to be at a more relaxing pace, along the scenic meandering Oregon Coast, like a second honeymoon perhaps. We'd stop for a leisurely visit with Al's sister Pauline and her husband Chuck in Tacoma, Washington if we could catch them home. We also had in mind to maybe go to Vancouver after Las Vegas, if we had a few days to spare and still make it home at the end of the month for our business month end.

Traveling with Al was never boring. I settled back to enjoy his state of constant awe at the beauty and wonders of nature and the marvels of man-made structures and bridge designs en route. He kept watch for historical sites and roadside plaques, each one a learning opportunity. It was never just about reaching a destination. It was all about creating and discovering adventures along the scenic routes. For this trip my desired travelling style was different. I preferred well-traveled, most direct routes from point A to point B to get this over with and onto the lovely trip home. Our trip conversations often would sound like this (no disrespect to Al). If I said "I don't feel good about going this way," he countered with, "Roads have to go somewhere. If there's a way in, there's a way out." And when I disagreed and said, "But we're not at home. We don't know these roads!" he would respond with, "What's to know? We're not on the moon!" I was nervous on this day because we were on a trip to a place where I had never gone before. I consoled myself, by thinking to myself that I was just being unreasonable. I needed to put it out of my mind.

Just before the US border crossing, Al took a moment to phone and chat with our long-time friend Dave who was taking our business calls while we were away. On the US side, we crossed through Washington state and most of Oregon, on Interstate 84, before we needed to refuel. We stopped at a gas station and convenience store visible from the highway in Baker City, Oregon. "Look, we are on camera," I said. A video surveillance camera captured us casually browsing, taking our sweet time, and in no obvious trouble. We picked up a few snacks that we consumed right away.

With a full tank of gas we re-entered the highway to carry on toward the Idaho state line. It was just a two-hour drive to Boise, Idaho, the logical place to stop for our first overnighter. We had plenty of daylight left. Between Baker City and Boise I suggested that since we had an early start on our day, we should stop in Boise for the night and go to church in the morning, and then carry on. But Al was not one bit tired. He brimmed with energy and wanted to keep going. I reasoned with Al until he agreed to at least a quick pit stop and lunch. We pulled over at a highway café and we went in to enjoy a side of nachos and sit a while. The nachos were so terrible we could hardly eat them. Al paid for them with cash. Walking back to the van I asked, "Why did you use cash and not a credit card? We wanted to save the US money for Las Vegas." "You're right, I wasn't thinking," he said. Later that proved to be detrimental!

Soon after the nacho stop, we continued our journey, on interstate 84. Nearing the turnoff toward Boise I pointed out a nice-looking motel with a vacancy sign. I knew I was being a nag, but I was desperate for a real break. "That would be a great place to pull over and call it a day," I suggested. "We're not in any rush. Let's stop now, get a good rest and an early start tomorrow." This was when I learned of Al's surprise travel plan. A friend back home had told him about a town called Jackpot. Located in the northeastern corner of Nevada, this town was, his friend assured him, a great place to stay overnight on the way to Las Vegas. Another friend, also a seasoned Nevada traveler, endorsed the Jackpot recommendation. Al was sold. There was no use debating. We were going to hit Jackpot or bust. My heart was wounded! I sure hoped the stop would at least be interesting. I recently found out that the town got its official name Jackpot in 1959, after evolving from a modest highway stopover into an Old West-style resort destination. It holds the lure of the old frontier with business names like Cactus Pete's, Four Jacks, and Pair-a-Dice. Touted as a "high-desert jewel" the town is surrounded by a 6.3 million acre wilderness area—Humboldt National Forest—the largest national forest in the lower forty-eight states. Local Idahoans and Nevadans know not to go up into the wilderness unprepared or alone, and never in winter! Tourists passing through have no idea!

I had made my best case for stopping early in Boise and against pushing on to Jackpot. Getting in late meant we probably wouldn't have time for a nice dinner, or maybe no dinner at all. Everything would be closed. But Al was too charged up to hear me. We drove through Mountain Home, but logic did not seem to register as he turned south on Highway 51. I was ticked. That's it! I was going to have a nap! Complaining wasn't going to help, and besides, if I rested along the straight stretch of highway ahead I'd be in good shape to take over the wheel when Al would eventually get tired.

Chapter Two

Stranded and Alone

I don't know how long I slept. It must have been quite a while because when I woke up we were long past the straight stretch of highway. The moment I opened my eyes and looked over at Al I could tell something was wrong. His face was tense and strained. "Where are we?" I asked. Al admitted that he wasn't too sure, and that wasn't good because we were almost out of gas. He thought there would have been a gas station long before now. He had been keeping his eyes peeled but there was no sign of a turnoff to Jackpot. We pulled out our roadmap to get our bearings and look for a connecting route. Our map showed only one way to Jackpot. We didn't have the forestry road map for more details. We would have to turn around and backtrack all the way we had come, back up Highway 51 and across Idaho, on Interstate 84 east, before turning south on Highway 93 to Jackpot. That distance would be too many miles with our already almost empty gas tank! We needed to find a gas station and a quicker way to Jackpot!

We consulted our new GPS unit. Just a few months earlier we had purchased the navigation system for a trip to Edmonton after attending my father's funeral in Terrace BC in December 2010. We found it helpful and easy to use on unfamiliar city streets. For the Nevada trip we intended to rely on our printed highway map. The GPS was with us only to navigate the streets of Las Vegas. We had no choice but to try the GPS. We were desperate! Al punched in Jackpot

Nevada as our destination. Based on our current coordinates a route to the east showed up. We wouldn't have to backtrack north after all. We could carry on, watching for a gas station that had to be not far up ahead. There was still no road sign to Jackpot but we kept on driving as the GPS guided.

Soon we were on a country gravel road. We came to an intersection. We had to make a choice. We chose Taylor Creek three miles, hoping it was a town. Before long, the country road turned into a rutted trail that got rougher as we went. This was not good! This was more than a rough patch. "There has to be a way out. There always is," said Al. I was not convinced! By now it was dark. I was terrified! Cinched between steep banks and sheer drop-offs, we watched for a place to turn around. Our trusty rear-wheel drive 2000 Astro van rumbled over jagged exposed rocks and around sharp twists. Al had to stop at intervals to remove boulders and debris from the trail. There must have been a recent storm.

I was praying without ceasing! It was impossible to turn around. I was frightened and upset but tried to keep the growing panic from showing on my face. My heart went out to Al as he concentrated on keeping the van moving. He had broken out in a cold sweat. I had never ever seen him so agitated. "Lord, help us!" he shouted aloud. I didn't dare voice the words, "we're going to die!", that screamed inside my head. We bumped and crawled along for a long time before we spied an encouraging sign: fresh tire tracks. "See," Al exclaimed, "looks like a four-by-four truck came through here recently so this has to be a way to somewhere!" Our hope was to find a cabin or a ranch house up ahead. Al declared, "We're going to get to Vegas. We're going to make it! I'm not wasting this trip!" The tire tracks eased our sense of alarm but not for long. Very soon they mysteriously disappeared without a trace. Still unable to turn around we inched onward. We had no other option. Furious at himself, Al shouted, "I'm so dumb." He tacked on a couple of choice words, "We're screwed!" Talking silently to myself, I voiced a desperate prayer: "If we can't turn back Lord, please help us to keep on moving forward." My thoughts were racing! "We'll get through this. Everything will be fine. We're going to be okay." With every passing minute and for every slow motion mile we kept watch for a place, any place, fit for a turn around. We pressed on as it grew darker, getting on to 9:00 p.m. We tried to phone for help but there was no cell service.

Things couldn't get any worse, or so we thought right up until everything got worse. Without warning the van hit a hidden trap. All four tires sank into a deep mud hole in a low spot on the trail, stopping the van cold and holding it in a powerful grip. Our terrible reality was all too clear. How could this happen? We simply couldn't believe it. In a state of shock, we sat paralyzed, at a complete loss. "Are you mad at me?" Al asked after a long silence. My thoughts soared. You bet I was mad. How could I not be? If he had listened to me, everything would be different. We were missing out on a nice dinner and a comfortable sleep. I could have piled on a mountain of blame but that wouldn't have fixed anything or made either of us feel better. Besides, I felt partly responsible. "I shouldn't have napped. I should have stayed awake to help navigate," I told him. In my tired and anxious state, I didn't dare say any more.

Several more attempts to use our cell phone proved futile. Al climbed out from the driver's seat, stepped across the mud hole and circled the van to survey the damage. There was hard digging work ahead all right. He could hardly wait to get at it. I was more worried about his health and safety than about being stranded for one night. "Let's wait it out until morning," I said. "We're hungry and tired. Why don't we just have a bite to eat and try to get some rest?" Our hearts were heavy. We willed ourselves to snack on a handful of crackers, washed down with a shared can of 7UP. There wasn't anything more we could do. We each stretched our tiny quilts over our shoulders and did our best to settle down. It was dark and quiet in the middle of nowhere but sleep was virtually impossible. We were very cold and so discouraged! I didn't dare say a word. There was nothing good to say. I know we were both praying silently with desperation! My mind replayed the perfect storm of wrong turns and faulty decisions that got us here. It was good we didn't know that night how much worse our troubles were about to get. A scripture verse from the book of Isaiah came to mind. I was slightly encouraged. While sensing that we were in big trouble, I hung on to the promise it contained. "*Fear thou not; for I am with thee; be not dismayed; for I am thy God; I will strengthen thee; yea, I will help thee;" (Isaiah 41:10, KJV)*

Things don't always look better in the morning. In the harsh reality of our Sunday morning we faced the awful truth head on. We were stuck in such an unimaginably bad place—we may as well have landed on the moon. We nibbled on a scant breakfast of Trail Mix and crackers, too distraught to eat much. Al was anxious to get started on digging. In normal times he enjoyed an earth-moving challenge but there was no joy in this mud trap. The heavy gumbo trap was unlike any Al had ever encountered. His only digging tool, our aluminum lightweight snow shovel, was quite flimsy for the impossible task. Al had to stop every few minutes to straighten out the bent, twisted metal with stone-age tools—the rocks nearby. It seemed futile to dig mud when more mud poured right back in. He jacked up the back wheels to open up space to drop in boulders that we hauled over from nearby and placed them under and around the tires, hoping they could create enough traction for the van to back onto a dryer section of the trail. After furious hours of sweat and tears, the stage was set. Al climbed into the driver's seat and started the engine. I cheered from the sidelines, held my breath and prayed. This was a do-or-die moment. He shifted into low gear and applied slow steady pressure to the accelerator pedal. The tires spun mud out into a soupy mess. It was hopeless.

If we were ever going to get out of here and back to civilization it would have to be on foot. We knew it was risky. We didn't have proper hiking boots to walk out and we didn't have winter survival gear to stay. We were determined to give it our best try. Following the GPS instructions to walk forward and find Mountain City seemed like a good plan at the time. The warmish weather held steady through the morning. At least that much seemed to be working in our favour. So before noon, we layered up in our extra shirts and warmer jackets. Al put on his work boots that he had expected to be exploring the trade show in. I had only lightweight shoes and dressy heeled boots that would have been perfect for wandering in Las Vegas. My best footwear solution here was Al's pair of oversized rubber boots. Even with three pairs of socks on, my feet and ankles wobbled. We packed our small backpacks with water bottles and the few snacks we still had. Al suggested we take pictures of each other before we ventured out very far. We aren't smiling in those pictures. The camera captured the deep sadness and despair we could not hide. We left the camera in the van for the boys, just in case.

Taking one last look at our desolate van, we started our walk into the unknown. At first we felt quite hopeful. Surely, sooner or later, we'd cross paths with a rancher or a hunter's cabin. It was slow going from the start. We trudged up long hills and down slushy inclines. On uneven ground, we groped our way over sharp rocks and slippery debris. It looked like the aftermath of a season of snow and heavy rains. Al walked on a bit ahead to scout out the best steps to take. He coaxed and encouraged me along. He always was the best *picker-upper*. I kept my boots moving as he called me on. "Just a little farther, around this corner," then "on the other side of this hill." On and on! "We'll see smoke or lights any time now," building hope upon hope as we carried on. In his younger years, Al walked his family's trap line and later he scaled mountainous terrain for the forest industry. In more recent years he measured his work sites by pacing steps. His outdoor tracking skills were put to good use now, to mark distances by pegging sticks in the ground, making sure we could find our way back if need be.

We slogged on for a few hours. We tried for cell service again but no luck! Discouragement set in. There was no house or cabin in sight, not even the slightest sign of human presence. We grew hot and sweaty from the exertion while the air grew cooler and the cloud cover thickened. Freezing rain started and snow would not be far behind. At about seven kilometers, I could not go on. My left knee was in bad shape, unbearably painful from sloshing around in the oversize boots. I rested briefly. We hated to retreat but we agreed that there was no choice. We had to turn back. Al was so visibly upset that I was afraid he would have a heart attack on the spot, and then what would happen to us? The long trek back was even tougher than the hard-going forward. It was like cross-country skiing on a muddy downhill. Pain shot through my knee at every stride. We made it back but it didn't feel like victory. It felt like utter defeat. How could this be our life? Disheartened, we cried out for our Lord to help us. We felt foolish that this was really happening! So what could we do now?

Al didn't quit! He gave one last effort piling more rocks in and yes—traction! For a brief moment, all that hard work seemed to be paying off. He skillfully eased the groaning vehicle up and out of the bog onto the trail's shoulder. But what good was it anyway? We couldn't go anywhere! It was still too muddy and we had only a few drops of fuel left. Al felt we needed to get off the trail, like we were being rude or something! Half-heartedly, we made one last-ditch effort to free the van. Our elation was cut short. Under the thin grassy veneer a worse trap lurked. Al proceeded to back around the soft muddy area. In a blink, however, the van slipped sideways off the shoulder and into the ditch against the side of the hill. The muddy bog sucked it down deeper than the wheel wells. This was total disaster. Al had given his best fight but now he had to concede. The mud had won. Nothing short of a tow truck with a heavy duty winch could pull the van free this time. Our day ended in physical pain and a sense of sheer disbelief. Desperate for sleep that night and restless and cold, we eventually settled down to sleep only because of extreme weariness.

Monday dawned with no bright solution in sight. We nibbled on bits of trail mix (rationing severely) as we began our day with a Bible reading and devotional. We entrusted the day into the Lord's good hands. Back to ground zero. We had to get help. Our cell phone still had a bit of charge left but we couldn't pick up reception in the lowland between the hills. Al climbed to a different hilltop, even farther away from our mud spot. He got a weak signal and quickly dialed 911. The call was answered. He detected a faint voice and read out our GPS coordinates but the signal faded and died. He had been so close to summoning help! He climbed to an even higher elevation and again caught a weak signal before losing the connection. Our final mayday had failed.

Al then came up with a desperate plan. After trying to build a fire with wet scrub brush sticks, he suggested setting the van on fire so smoke could be seen by farmers or ranchers in the area, or maybe even by a search party. I put an instant kibosh on that scheme. I reminded him that our van was needed, just as it was, on four wheels. It was our only shelter and protection. We couldn't survive without it. "Besides," I told him, "there are no searchers. No one is out looking for us because no one knows we're lost. Everyone thinks we've arrived in Las Vegas by now."

We spent the afternoon collecting branches for me to build a much needed fire. Al was planning to go for help the next day. "So let's look at things you'll need here until I get back," said Al. My crash course in Wilderness Survival 101 began with a lesson in harnessing solar power. He demonstrated how to melt snow by placing our only container, a medium-sized Rubbermaid bin, on the van's metal roof in the day and taking it in at night. Then he showed me ways to stay safe from wild animals and how to get a fire going with the magnifying glass that we always carried in our glove compartment for reading maps. He demonstrated with the damp branches but the flame extinguished quickly.

We had scouted out our trapped corner of the world and discovered a snow-covered creek, really just a run-off ditch, just a short hiking distance downhill. He led me on the trail to point out the best spot to get drinking water. I would have to collect water only if the snowfalls stopped. He planned to be back in a few days, long before the end of snow season. To level out the precariously tilted van, he jacked up the back corner and packed large rocks underneath to keep it steady.

Al picked up the flimsy snow shovel and set to work digging ten small holes along the sloped hill behind the van. "These are outdoor latrines," he instructed me, "one for each day until I get back. You won't need all ten. But if, for any reason, I'm gone longer, you'll have to dig more." I protested, "why do I have to do that? This is open rangeland for cattle and all kinds of animals." "The human scent attracts them," he explained, "especially bears." He had my attention! He was well aware of my lifelong fear of bears. "Besides," he added, "it's in the Bible, really!" No doubt it would have been a smart practice for forty years of wandering in the wilderness.

He had one more piece of parting advice. "In the mornings, before daylight, he said, start up the van and let it run for a couple of minutes and turn on the lights in case someone's out there. Maybe a helicopter or plane will happen to fly over. Do that every morning as long as the gas and the battery hold out."

We turned to our GPS unit and wondered if we could trust it since it's what got us here in the first place. But everything had to be tried. If Al could get high enough on a hill to detect coordinates it could possibly give us a plan to get out. The signal was too weak. We recharged the unit overnight off the van's battery power and gave it another try in the morning. That was enough trouble for one day. Al gave the van tires a couple of good hard kicks. "Stupid, stupid!" he muttered. I understood his frustration. I stood by helpless, anxious about his blood pressure, for his sake and mine too. There was no way in the world I could imagine surviving out here if something happened to him.

Our day was spent. We sure needed a good sleep. Hungry and tired we ate a small nibble of our rations, prayed desperate prayers, and fell asleep. The night was colder than before. I hardly slept a wink on that dark night of my soul. My knee throbbed with pain and I was cramped and cold. But mostly I stayed awake to gather my thoughts and talk things over with Jesus. He had always helped us out with our struggles before and there was no doubt this was our toughest yet! I was clinging to hope. Through the dark hours I thought about the string of decisions that led to our disaster. I wondered, if we made more mistakes, were we going to die on this mountain? I listened to Al's deep regular breathing, glad he was getting a good sound sleep. He had earned it. He needed to be well-rested for what was still ahead. Al and I looked at our dire situation differently. My thinking was that it was best to be patient and stay with the van. But it was simply against Al's nature to sit and wait around. He was wired for action. He was sure he could make it to Mountain City to get help in three days.

Chapter Three

The Terrible Parting

At sunrise on Tuesday March 22, we woke up to about six inches of fresh snow but it was sunny and warmish. My hunch was confirmed. After considering every angle and weighing every pro and con, we circled back to a same conclusion. Help hadn't come to us so Al would go out to bring it in. He figured it was fifty-fifty odds for walking out and rounding up a rescue crew with a goal of being back within days, a week at the most. Staying with the van in the hope that someone would show up, given the road conditions and time of year, he calculated our chances as slim to none. We could not wait any longer. With every passing day, our meager food supply dwindled. We had barely enough food for one person to last a week. I'm not going to just sit here," he declared. "We need to be out of this mess in a day or two to catch at least the last day of the convention!" Al was still determined to get to the equipment show. I just wanted to go home!

With milder weather and snow melting on the ground, the timing seemed right for a trek out. Al still had strength and stamina to spare. If not now, it might be never. It just made sense to try, so he prepared to do what most any man would do. We sized up and divided our tiny bit of nuts and candy. I kept the small bag of trail mix and candy. He packed a couple handfuls of chocolate covered almonds and a few hard candies. That would give boosts of energy for the endurance test ahead.

A walk to Mountain City, the closest community showing up on our map, could take up to three days—faster if he came across a ranch or hunter's cabin. He promised to stick to the trails, guided by the GPS route. He wrote it on a paper for himself and for me also in case I was rescued first then I could send them to find Al. He set himself one clear goal: "I'm going to walk until I can't walk anymore."

My knee was so badly swollen I couldn't possibly attempt even a short walk. "You know I can't go with you," I said, hoping that might slow down his thinking. "I know," he said with a sadness that brought us both to tears. For my sake, he perked up. He kept his brave face on, but I read his eyes. He read my eyes too. I couldn't hide my anxiety about the grueling journey and my worries about the toll it would take on his health, never mind the risk of death!

For thirty eight years, we started every day on high ground, meeting personally with our Father God. Sadly we were not comfortably seated at our kitchen table enjoying a hearty breakfast and coffee. Here we were shivering in the seats of our land-locked Astro Van, washing down a little nibble of trail mix with icy cold water. But as always, we turned to "Our Daily Bread" devotional booklet. The reading for Tuesday March 22, 2011, was titled *How to Bloom.*" That sounded promising. We read the scripture passage from (*1 Peter 4:12, KJV*): *"Beloved, think it not strange concerning the fiery trial which is to try you, as though some strange thing happened to you; but rejoice…"* We knew that precisely-timed message was not a coincidence, but it was also not the scripture we would have chosen for this morning. We didn't want to be tested and tried by a fiery trial! What happened to us was a strange thing all right and what we wanted was the fastest and easiest way out. We pressed on to read the whole commentary. "God wants to loosen the things that can choke our lives and that prevent us from radiating joy. To do this, He sometimes has to allow pain and trouble—trials that help stir the soil of our lives." We were in the soil-stirring business. The metaphor struck home.

We needed something more to steady our little lifeboats. Al picked up his King James Bible and thumbed the well-worn pages to a favorite passage in the Gospel of Matthew. He read Jesus's words to me. *"Therefore I say unto you, take no thought for your life, what ye shall eat or what ye shall drink; nor yet for your body, what ye shall put on. Is not the life more than meat, and the body than raiment? Behold the fowls of the air: for they sow not, neither do they reap, nor gather into barns; yet your heavenly Father feedeth them. Are ye not much better than they?" (Matt 6:25, KJV).* Those words anchored us. We couldn't see God's purpose or plan in this storm, but we could trust His heart through it all. Al took my trembling hands and prayed, "Jesus, please don't let Rita be afraid. Take care of her until I return. Thank you for watching over both of us. Thank you for staying with us." And then I bravely prayed, holding his hardworking hands, "Dear Lord, thank you for going with Al. Guide him and keep him safe along the way. Help him get there and back quickly." Our hearts aching, we embraced each other and we cried silently. I'm certain my heart ached on that morning more than all my lifetime strung together. Our last hug had to end. On the surface I appeared calm and composed. I loved Al too much to make his tough choice even tougher, so I kept all my inner screaming to myself, "Al, don't leave me here alone! I won't know what to do!"

It was about 9:00 a.m. My head shifted into a kind of slow motion surreal state. I watched him slip from the driver's seat. I saw him plant his feet firmly on the ground. He adjusted his small blue backpack and squared his shoulders. He beamed that endearing boyish smile and gave a final blessing, "God will be with you," he paused, "and me too." And then my best friend, my husband, turned onto the trail and took his first steps away from me. Sitting in the passenger's seat, I watched every stride. Not for an instant did I take my eyes off his back. Before rounding the last hillside, he turned around and blew me a kiss. My eyes blurred with tears and in one more blink he disappeared. As soon as he was safely out of range, I came apart at the seams. "No! This can't be! I can catch up if I run. I can get him to change his mind. I can beg him to come back!" But I wouldn't do that even if I could have run. He needed to go and I needed to believe he would come back soon. The fearful thought that I would never see him again crept close. I shoved it away. "This cannot be real! It has to be just the worst kind of nightmare!"

I eased myself out of my seat onto the ground. Favoring my injured knee, I paced gingerly back and forth on the rutted trail in front of me. Through the morning hours, I never stopped praying, "Lord, keep him safe. Don't let him suffer." I am sure his earnest prayer was one of his favorite verses as he hiked the difficult trail ahead. *"But they that wait upon the Lord shall renew their strength; they shall mount up with wings as eagles; they shall run, and not be weary; and they shall walk, and not faint."* (Isaiah 40:31, KJV)

After a midafternoon rest, tired of the flat circuit, I limped over to the peak of a little hill and looked far out in the direction that Al went, hoping I might catch a glimpse of his progress. But all I saw was a vast sea of hills, one after another in every wild direction. My new aloneness felt like an arrow in my heart. I retreated to the van to make a half hearted entry in my journal. I wrote it in block capital letters, although I'm not sure why. My normal handwriting style is cursive. Perhaps this was a subconscious effort to cope with emotional trauma. As the days passed the printing was a morning ritual and seemed to be a duty I should not neglect.

I promised myself that for three days and three nights I would be brave. Then he would be back and all would be well. If anyone had been watching me, they would have thought how strong I was and how well I was handling things, but I was very nervous. I needed to settle in. It took quite an effort to make my nest as cozy as possible with little to work with, certainly barely enough for the cold nights. I dreaded the thought of nights without Al. I was running out of words to pray and felt close to a panic attack. I was thinking about when David in the scriptures was crying out to God in *Psalm 22, 1–8, KJV*. He was desperate! As I read more, I was calmed by the words. David felt abandoned by God but he knew he could trust God no matter what.

Finally, the sad day was mercifully over. I had a shelter from the heavy blizzard that lasted all through the night. That ditch against the hill now proved to be a good protection from the blowing winds. I could hardly handle thinking about Al out there, only God knew where. The darkness of the night and the noise of the howling winds were disconcerting. I drifted into the great relief of forgetful sleep.

Chapter Four

Ice Hearts to Feathered Friend

Before daylight on my stormy first night alone, I was startled awake by the sound of an airplane in the distance. Then I remembered Al's parting advice. In the mornings, just before daylight, until the battery wore down or the gas ran out, he said I should start up the van and turn on the headlights because someone might notice the light and come to check it out. I quickly turned on the ignition to clear the frost, flicked on the headlights and hoped for a miracle. Shivering in the icy air I sank back into my uncomfortable front seat to wait for the welcome relief of some heat if even by a degree. Wasn't it just days earlier when Al and I agreed that the muddy trail signaled a spring thaw? But that was just a tease. The high-elevation winter conditions weren't over, not by a long shot. Winter was back with a vengeance that night. The temperature dropped and there was another six inches of fresh snow by morning.

As the van idled and the air warmed, my eyes were drawn to the ice-coated windshield. Jack Frost had been hard at work. To my amazement, I noticed a clear pattern etched into the frost, as defined as the brushstrokes of a master painter. I saw two perfectly-shaped hearts linked together, as if holding hands. I stared in awe, transfixed by the still-life etching. "This is a message from you, isn't it Al," I said out loud, my breath forming a cloud in the frosty air. "You're telling me you're okay, right? You're praying for me right now, aren't you?" Wow! This was certainly an original way to send a love note! As the windshield continued to warm I had to be certain I wasn't dreaming. I leaned forward and reached out my hand to touch the crystal artwork. My fingers lightly traced the cold heart edges that were already beginning to soften. Before my eyes the ice image changed. Crystal by crystal the two linked hearts formed into one large, exquisitely-shaped heart. I was stunned. Gradually the large heart melted and vanished into thin air. My ice show was fleeting but the memory is a forever treasure. In the crystal clear language of the heart, I was sure that Al had pledged his love to me again and I had watched our love link together with the boundless love of God. I turned off the ignition and wrapped up tight again to catch more sleep before morning, comforted to know Al was okay and would be back in just a couple more days.

There were many more frosty nights and frozen windshields after that first lonely night but never again did ice images form. Once was enough. I understood the message. In the string of lost days and weeks to come, when he did not come back, I often reflected on the meaning of the crystal hearts. Over time I came to accept that the hearts could have been Al's farewell. If his first night in the wilderness was his last night on earth, he had sent me a parting gift, a last kiss. I saw a picture of his love, heart-to-heart upon an icy windshield. No matter what happened, love had it all covered, Al's love and God's love.

Hours later, still half asleep, my ears picked up a tiny cheerful sound. I opened my eyes and turned my weary head to look out at my side mirror. I wasn't alone! There I spied a tiny gray and blue-tinted bird, perched jauntily and chirping boldly, as if she owned the morning. I slowly rolled my window down, just a crack, careful not to scare off my company. But I didn't have to worry. The cheeky little creature didn't flinch. Singing in the chilly air, my tiny winged visitor treated a rapt audience of one to a striking solo performance. My heart was so captured by the beautiful notes that I forgot for a moment about my dire state of affairs. Even the gray-brown hills, gilded overnight by a sparkling snow-like fleece, looked beautiful. It was just the two of us and no one else. So I decided it wouldn't appear crazy to sing along with my new friend. I chirped in for our first sunrise duet.

My miniature friend never left, not from that first morning on. She was there to greet me with a song every morning. She brought me noonday and evening songs, and she made cameo appearances whenever I was in most need of a friend. I soon realized she was a gift from God. By the muted colors I identified my bluebird friend as a female. Two to three inches long from her top feather to the tip of her tail, she was mostly gray-brown with hints of pale blue in her wings. When the sun shone her blue patches showed up brighter, as if tinged by the brush of an artist. She had a splash of orange feathers on her chest and her bill was entirely jet-black. Her male counterparts were unbelievably sky-blue, with even more striking colors on the wings and tail.

She was alone. "Are you lonely, little bird?" I asked. "You're not off with all the other birds. Are you here because you know I'm lonely too?" On my walks, there she was nestled in bushes nearby or rustling on waving tufts of grass. Every day, in every kind of weather, she was miraculously and marvelously there. She seemed to sense my needs. When I felt sad or discouraged she just happened to appear out of the blue to offer a snippet of joy. Her constant presence reminded me to trust God. Countless times I thanked Him for the gift of her light-hearted company. My bird listened to my troubles as I believe the Lord did too, and she consoled me in her best chirping voice. Somehow we understood each other. I watched her closely. It gave me courage to hear her singing just as cheerfully on stormy and gloomy days as on the few sunny blue-sky days.

If I had had a birding book I could have officially identified her species. Now I know I had the honor of befriending the official state bird of Idaho and Nevada —a Mountain Bluebird. A book would have told me what I learned from first-hand observation. Mountain Bluebirds are easy to find by driving high elevation rural roads. They can be spotted perching in the open range country and, as I discovered, they are not shy of humans. My bird was an air-lifted gift of love. Al knew how much I dreaded being alone. I like to believe he asked God to send me a friend. He may not have been thinking of a friend with feathers. But it wouldn't be the first time God gave a special angel assignment to a bird. I remembered the last living words Al and I had read together were, "take no thought for your life… Look at the fowls of the air." I took that admonition literally and looked at my carefree bird of the air. She showed me what trusting God for today and not worrying about tomorrow looked like. I never introduced myself and I never gave her a name. We were just two lonely blue patches in a gray-brown world, singing where no one but God could hear. I sang many songs to cheer myself up. I had a hard time remembering words to familiar hymns and choruses, so I would make them up hoping that they would come back to me.

Chapter Five

Survival Mode

After meeting my feathered friend that first morning, I knew I had to toughen up and get out there in the cold! The next several days after Al left were cold and stormy. Keeping warm was impossible, but just enough to survive was my hope and prayer each night. I curled up in the reclining passenger's seat with my two child-size quilts stretched around me. For a change of position, I would lay on the back seats, to adjust my kinked neck or aching back from the night before.

Every day, I told myself this is the day that help will be here. But in reality, I had to make an action plan for survival, even though I was anxious for a rescue! When troubles hit, there are two options—find a way out or make a plan to endure. Al had put his best effort into finding a way out. Now, I had to find a way to endure and not lose hope. I had to believe that things were going to work out. I just had to be patient. After a few nights passed, I said to myself, "The worst scenario: Al might be gone for a week, and this will all be over soon." I thought that the more I slept, the more energy I would conserve until my rescuers arrive.

My daily challenge was to remain positive. That was not always easy. I thought about Al and how he might be doing. I still didn't want to believe that he died out there. I tried thinking of every scenario possible to have hope upon hope that he somehow was still alive. He could be about half way by now. If he came across a ranch he might already be on his way back with help. His legs were probably getting tired, but that's okay because he would just stop and rest awhile and carry on. I pictured him right on track, safe and sheltered, not lost and not suffering. I hung on to that hope for dear life! Many times over the next days, however, dark thoughts slipped in. Is he okay or did he freeze to death on that first night? I became conscious of a strange reality. At this point, no one had a clue that we were lost and in deep trouble! Everyone pictured us having the greatest time in Vegas. If only they were right!

After a week went by, I welcomed the sun going down each evening. I was ready for my escape from my intense reality. I would fall asleep shortly after dark, but not before my feathered friend would sing to me her good-night melody. She was my cheerleader! And by now, I could look forward to her cheerful wake-up call in the morning! I soon had a routine: wake up, get out and freshen up, and brush my teeth. I would hang out my two bright-colored damp quilts on my windows to air them out and also use them as a visible flag in case anyone was searching for us. My daily ritual was to read the Bible and to pray in an audible voice. I nibbled my trail mix ration slowly. At less than a tablespoon a day, I figured I could stretch it to five breakfasts but I soon realized that I should cut back to a teaspoon a day, then it may last as long as two weeks.

During my first week, I was able to melt snow in a "Rubbermaid" container open to the warmth of the afternoon sun, on the roof of my van. Later, when it only snowed a small amount during the nights, I went for walks to a nearby drainage ditch to get water to drink. I had promised myself that as long as I lived, I would make the effort to get my water. I was so glad that I had six empties to use. I carefully poured the top portions of the collected water, after a settling time, into Al's metal coffee travel mug. That way, I didn't have to look at the soupy brown liquid in the small clear plastic bottles. I enjoyed the aroma of coffee that still lingered in his well-used mug. The murky water had kind of a sweet mineral taste to it.

Each day I would read inside my van for hours at a time, but I would also get out and walk around a little on the afternoons that weren't too rainy or windy. Often, I would read and pray myself to sleep. I could sleep whenever I wanted to. I would nap every afternoon as long as I could, just to keep cozy and help the time pass. When I slept, I forgot about being hungry and anxious for a rescue.

That day soon came, April 5th, when my little bag of Trail Mix was empty. I ate the few remaining seeds, the one final almond and the single yogurt covered cranberry—so tasty! I had eaten less nuts each day to make it last. That was good news to me. It meant this must be the day for my rescue. I packed my bags, so I would be ready to go at a moment's notice. I stretched my legs with a little walk around. I prayed and reminded the Lord I was ready to go home. Later in the afternoon because no one showed up, it crossed my mind that God had far more serious things to tend to than my mud jam. But surely, if a rescue was his plan, it had to come soon because I couldn't survive much longer. I was hungry and weary. All I had left was my fish oil and candy. I rationed myself to just two fish oil capsules a day, one in the morning and one at night. At around noon, before getting water, I would eat one candy to give myself a little energy boost for the walk down to the drainage ditch.

On that April 5th afternoon, I heard my mother's voice clearly in my head, "God's word is our food." I remembered her saying that when I was a child. We were having our Bible reading from "Our Daily Bread" devotional book before school as we always did. One of my brothers protested that morning. He said, "Why can't we eat first? I am hungry!" Her answer that day stayed with me. For a brief moment, I felt near to Mom. What a comfort that was to me that day! I knew that was not a literal statement but I took it in faith and declared it to God in a prayer of commitment. With all my heart I prayed to Jesus, "Your word is my food!" I believed it! I understood it to be my present comfort and assurance even though my stomach was not fed.

I still kept a close watch for any new ideas for food every day. I tried a nibble of almost every green plant that sprouted after the snow melted. Most made me feel sick and nauseous. One kind, very short-lived, was red and tiny like Alfalfa sprouts. I saw the birds eating them. So I nibbled on them for a few days. But then another snowstorm came and they were gone. The wildlife probably finished them.

One day, I noticed a thumping and scratching noise under my van. I heard it every night for a few weeks. As we used to raise rabbits for meat on our ten-acre farm in Terrace, British Columbia, I recognized the smell of rabbit urine. I was dreaming of one day catching some of those little bunnies and having shish-kebabs over a nice warm fire, but that never happened! There was no food to be had. I guess the bunnies ran off as soon as they were able. I didn't mind sharing that space as long as it wasn't skunks.

I often imagined a delicious plate of my favorite foods, like a plate of hot steamy macaroni and cheese or a bowl of creamy tomato soup with a grilled-cheese sandwich! I prayed that the Lord would miraculously nourish me, as if I had eaten the meal that I had been craving, trusting that he would sustain me as long as he saw fit.

I had reasons to be thankful every day. I was grateful for the basic comforts in my present shelter. I was protected and dry. It was the bare necessities but I was still alive. Counting blessings wasn't new to us. Al and I had often taken time out before our evening prayers, to reflect on the good life we shared—our healthy family, our wonderful friends and our profitable business, that met our family's needs and made it possible to help others meet theirs.

Chapter Six

Bone-Chilling Battles

Memories consumed my thoughts for hours every day. A blessing for sure! This was a rest from my grave reality in the present. My whole life was being replayed before me. Memories from my life cushioned me from the daily battles at hand. One night, a couple of days after Al left, I awakened from a deep sleep. I thought the deafening *chop, chop* sounds were just part of a strange nightmare. But the noise grew closer and louder until it shook me wide awake. I sat up and peered out into blinding bright lights. When my eyes adjusted, I made out the outline of a giant helicopter. It was flying low, very close by. I threw off my blankets, tore open the door, and scurried out to stand beside the van. The shiny black helicopter was in a holding position, hovering over by the creek. On higher ground, I was almost at eye level. With fear and hope mixed together, I was thinking, "Why are they here? They must be looking for me! Al must have reached them and told them how to find me. This must be my rescue!"

I fumbled for my flashlight, switched it on, and waved it frantically back and forth, desperate to draw their attention. It was no use. My tiny light was swallowed up by their powerful lights. I clearly saw the silhouette of three men crouched in the open door of the helicopter with backpacks on. The chopper hovered for several seconds before the craft lifted and flew off into the night's black hole, never to reappear. Dejected and shivering, I retreated to my lost world and cried myself back to sleep.

The line between harsh reality and wishful thinking was wafer thin. Later in the clear light of dawn, I thought maybe the helicopter visit had been a dream. Long after the helicopter incident and after my rescue, I asked a friend with ties to the US military some questions about this helicopter sighting and found out that a military training camp may have conducted night exercises in that area of Nevada that night because that was common practice. I probably hadn't hallucinated, after all.

It snowed almost every night for the first week. The mountain air still screamed of winter. I was always cold. The first weeks were the coldest of the cold—day and night! The van was a virtual deep freeze on wheels. Frost formed on the windows and water bottles froze solid overnight. My breath formed icy puffs of air. Streams of frigid wind seeped through the van's front air vents, bringing an arctic touch. Two nights later I ripped my phone book into two thick slabs to place over the air vents. Al always liked to keep a phone directory in our vehicles. It was far from a perfect solution but the paper held some of the frost at bay.

Without the two small quilts I grabbed at the last minute before embarking on our journey, I would have frozen to death. They were literally a life-saver! These quilts were padded with llama wool, perfect quilts for our grandchildren's sleepovers. I covered them with a blue flannel "digger" design on the front and with plain bright red flannel on the back. Now the red and the blue blanket hugged my shivering body and warmed my heart. I was grateful for them, even though I was still cold! I wasn't going to let the frigid temperatures beat me! I had to be creative and resourceful with everything and anything on hand.

Even though I had layered Al's jean shirt and a thin windbreaker over my own clothes, it never seemed quite enough to feel comfortably warm. One of our "Rital" company toques fit snuggly around my head under the hood of my lightweight jacket. To keep my head warmer, I retrieved a safety pin from our first-aid kit to pin the hood tight under my chin. Two more safety pins held a toque on each foot over top of three pairs of socks in an attempt to keep my feet from freezing when the temperature dropped overnight. Even with these extra layers, some nights, I woke up to frozen toes. I was thankful for my first-aid kit with a few extras in it. The tube of joint pain cream sure came in handy to rub on my cold toes to warm them up so I could go back to sleep. I have permanent numbness on the bottom of my feet now. The surface of the skin feels like paper is pasted on it.

After the first week, my knee was not as swollen but every step was still painful. I came up with my own physiotherapy regime. I stood in the middle section of the van and balanced myself between two seats. For days in a row, I slowly rocked my bent leg back and forth. The moment came when I felt something in my disjointed knee snap into place. After that snap my knee was almost as good as new. I continued with that exercise to get my circulation going in the mornings after my cramped style each night.

One night during the first week, I had a scary nightmare about a black helicopter that landed right in front of my van. A gang of men armed with guns emerged and began walking toward me. I woke up from sleeping, almost fainted for fear but all was quiet. I scratched the frost off the window to peer out and be sure that it was just a dream. I had that same nightmare a couple nights before leaving on this trip and it made me really nervous about going! I had to pray in the middle of the night to get peace about even going on the trip. I don't really like leaving the country, probably because I had lived a very sheltered life growing up and hardly ever left my hometown.

Weeks went by and it was getting easier to get my courage up in the mornings. Enough of this, I decided. I may as well just appreciate the quiet. I actually recognized the growing peace I began to feel at night before falling asleep. "Look at the birds of the air" were the first words of good counsel Al and I had received from our Bible reading on the morning that he left me. So I watched my little bird friend and took note that she was not afraid. She was always totally content. Watching her, I had to admit, I was feeling quite fine too. I realized that none of my fearful thoughts came from the Lord. I once was told that the Bible tells us 365 times, one for each day, "Do not be afraid!" So I prayed for all my fears to be taken away. They didn't go quickly, but in stages, they all lost their grip.

On one particular morning, I woke up to the sight of massive elk gazing straight at me through the driver's side window. Eight large eyes looking at one pair of wide eyes staring back. Their curiosity apparently satisfied, they turned and moseyed off. They must have decided, and I agreed, that there was no cause to trouble each other. I appreciated the company of mice and rabbits and the elk that stopped by for cameo visits. I was so starved for companionship I didn't even mind the spiders.

I recall that on one night, I almost fainted from fear! It was a night when there was a thunder and lightning storm so loud, that I awoke out of my sleep with a jolt. The van windshield cracked! I felt a spasm of fear like a bolt of lightning hitting my heart. I sat up and shouted "Peace! Be still!" I shouted again, "Peace! Be Still!" I was not sure, in my half-asleep, not-quite-awake state, why I shouted that. Instantly, the storm moved away, the sounds faded and the night grew quiet. I trembled awhile and went back to sleep, now just the sound of gentle rain all around. I hummed the lullaby "Rock-a-Bye Baby," imagining myself being held and cuddled by Jesus. I fell back into a deep sleep.

In the morning when I woke up, I was disoriented and could not recall my name. I recognized everything around me, but was perplexed as to why I was here and who I was! I was stunned and frozen in time for a while. I looked in my purse and at my driver's license. Gradually, my memory came back clearly. I remembered my grim circumstances. I remembered that we were on a trip and had gotten lost and that my husband had gone for help but hadn't come back yet. I reconnected with my painful reality. Then the other pieces slowly fell into place. My emotional pain of missing Al came back. While looking in my purse, I also saw the photos of two of my grandchildren, Anyalee and Deklan. I held them close. I wished I could hug them. I remembered my three other grandchildren, but had no photos of them with me.

That storm taught me a big lesson. My Lord was with me and He was taking care of me. I carefully examined the windshield. It was still intact but badly cracked. There was a little dribble of water leaking through. Fear attacked me at other times but this time I was in awe. This called for full outright thanks and praise. The Lord truly became my best friend on this lonesome mountain in the middle of nowhere.

As time went on, if it wasn't snowing it was raining steadily most nights, pounding on the metal roof, while wild winds rocked the van from side to side. The clay soil never had a fighting chance to dry out. The van sank lower, swallowed up in sticky, ankle-deep sludge. Now water rushed around the van like a creek. I was worried that the van would slip off the rocks that Al had leveled so nicely for my comfort. It may not hold forever! I needed my shelter! It was all the protection I had, and I couldn't survive without it!

After days and weeks of horrible weather, I had much work to do. With the flimsy shovel, I dug a moat around my Astro castle. As many times as that overworked piece of tin got bent up, I bent it back into shape and kept on digging. My arms ached and my muscles burned with pain. Al would have been proud that I didn't give up. After that, the pooled water drained away. The jacked-up back corner of the van, by Al's good work and by miraculous grace, held firm.

The flat rocks that I had placed the first week at my side door, as a threshold, were not enough now. I found some old discarded fence posts and laid them at my side door entrance so I could scrape the mud off my boots before entering my makeshift home. I found a clump of wild flowering weed. After tasting it, I quickly spit it out, because it was bitter and probably not edible. I planted it beside my door to cheer myself because it was the only pretty thing around. I was thankful for any small comforts. It disappeared after a few days. Maybe the rabbits ate it all.

Our brown van was invisible, perfectly camouflaged in an environment of brown and gray as far as the eye could see. Several times I heard jets in the sky, probably from the Boise airport, but they were too far away to see. Twice, I saw a propeller plane fly far in the distance, just a pinpoint dot in the sky. At first, I shouted and waved hoping for someone to notice the person grounded down below. After many hope-dashed days, I saw no more. A bright orange or a white van might have been visible from above. In case tiny patches of color could be seen from above, and as long as it wasn't pouring rain,

I hung out my bright red and blue blankets and a bright florescent green vest on the hood of my van. They never did end up working as attention getters, but they were my colorful flags of hope, dancing bravely in the wind.

At one point, I had great hopes of building a big bonfire to once again feel warm. This became an obsession so I built a fire pit, circled it with rocks and then spent hours collecting twigs for kindling. When the rains stopped long enough, I even collected dried up cow patties for fuel. Those patties gave me reason to hope cattle may come along with a cowboy! The work gave me something purposeful to do. I felt warmer just thinking of all the things I would burn. If only everything in this woeful corner of the world wasn't so thoroughly soggy! I tried and tried for hours on end to laser focus solar power with my magnifying glass. Wisps of smoke and flame teased me but fire never did catch for longer than a few seconds. The day came when I accepted that building a bonfire was mission impossible! I put in half-hearted efforts for a while longer, and then stopped trying altogether. I wasn't giving up entirely, just giving myself a break until dryer days.

This brown-and-gray landscape was my world now and only God knew for how long. I didn't have everything I wanted, but I had the bare necessities, and I didn't actually need much. God helped me to think straight. I didn't face my troubles all at once. I faced them one at a time. Bit by bit, I did whatever small thing had to be done, in the moment. I made only short-range plans. When I got to the end of my rope and threw up my hands and asked, "What now?" He showed me what to do next. Simple solutions, for the moment, seemed to come out of the blue. With hardly a smidgen of wilderness experience or survival training, I managed.

Chapter Seven

Thoughts of Home

On April 10th, I wrote in my journal, "COLDEST NIGHT SO FAR, MID-MORNING, WARMED UP, SOGGY PUDDLES EVERYWHERE". I was so discouraged and wondered if I would ever get back home again. I missed my family and grandchildren. I couldn't imagine what they might be thinking happened to us! "Maybe they were assuming that we had driven off the highway somewhere. What a night mare!" I thought. I was quite worried about how our employees were going to be paid and how all the business responsibilities were being handled because Al and I were the only ones that worked in the office! Would they ever know what happened out here? If only I could phone home! I longed for this to be over! After a good cry, I told myself that I could do one more day. I held onto my dream of some person on an ATV accidently stumbling upon my patch of mud-land. That seemed to be the only way.

I sifted through family memories, like paging through a photo album. My heart went out to my mother who was familiar with grief. Only months back on December 24, 2010, she lost her husband, my dad. She also carried the grief of losing her eldest daughter, Suzanne, in a car accident at the age of forty-two. Now her youngest daughter and husband were missing and probably dead as far as anybody knew. I prayed for deep peace and comfort for her.

By April 24th (Easter that year), I was very weary of this break from my "busy life." I was homesick! I was sure the family would assume that we were dead by now. If only I could be home in time for Easter and we could put this nightmare behind us. I hoped and prayed that my sons and their families would be able to be together for the holiday week end. The memory of the aroma of turkey and gravy teased me momentarily. I had to dismiss that lovely thought and get back to survival mode. I spent many hours thinking about my grandchildren and the cute things they did and the special times we had together when they spent time with me. I longed to see them again and hoped that it would be in God's plan to grant mercy to our family and bring me home soon!

I thought about our long-time Pastor, Neil Allenbrand. Every Sunday a really meaningful sermon was expounded to us. I sure wished I could be a fly on the wall and not miss any of the sermons. If I could have, I would have heard the heartfelt prayers going out for us because we were mysteriously missing. I would have heard the media updates reported to the congregation about us and the ongoing search. Every Sunday in the confines of my mountain home on wheels I had my own little service and prayer. It usually ended with many tears. One Sunday I had a wonderful dream! I heard Pastor Neil's voice. He was preaching up a lively message! It was like I was there again. When I woke up, I was much encouraged. I spent the next hour praying for my friends at church and for Pastor Neil, that they would not lose faith in God because we were missing and probably presumed dead. I hoped that they would not give up praying for us to be found. Drifting off into memory lane was consoling and also gave me things to pray about. I thought about my prayer group friends, who met with us in our home every week. We had many dinners together and many precious times. I knew I could count on them to pray for us once they realized we were missing. They all knew we were due home on March 30 at the latest.

I missed our Church of the Nazarene and pictured the communion service that day, the first Sunday of May. I decided to join in again as I did last month for communion from a distance. Back at the van I prepared my communion table. Water served as wine, Christ's lifeblood poured out for me. Days earlier I had discovered a piece of a broken cracker at the bottom of a box that I was just about to crumple up and bury in the ground. I saved that little corner of a cracker for this special occasion. It served well to remember the bread of life, Christ's body, broken for me. I read the Last Supper scriptures, just the way we do together at church. "Do this in remembrance of me," Jesus told his friends before he laid down His life to show the world the full extent of our Heavenly Father's love. I remembered, with deep thanks, all the ways Jesus has loved me, from yesterday to forever. Nothing, not even isolation in the wilderness or death itself, could separate me from the height and depth and breadth of God's love.

I wondered how my dear friends, Rita and Dwight McGillis, were feeling right now. I was quite sure that they would be worried sick about us by now. I was very concerned for them! I prayed that God would comfort them in their sorrows and challenges. They had enough to bear already. Dwight was in his own battle—serious Cancer! Rita was the main care-giver for him now! Al and I had a habit of visiting with them weekly, enjoying good times together. Rita sent out a group email when she heard that we were missing.

"Dear friends and family,

Life has taken so many twists and turns in the last month or so. Our "bestest" friends, Albert and Rita Chretien have been missing for thirty days now. They were last seen on March 19, 2011, in Baker City, USA. A gallant effort was conducted on both sides of the border by law officials and private citizens alike to locate our friends. We now believe (although we don't want to) that they are with Jesus. Law officials also believe that now the investigation is for recovery. The most likely scenario is that Albert and Rita had an accident and went off the road. Regardless of what happened Dwight and I miss our friends very much. Just two days ago, after sewing in my sewing room, I felt a need for a cup of coffee. As was our practice, I went upstairs to call my friend to have "phone" coffee with her. The phone was in my hands and I was ready to dial when I realized that she wasn't there. I miss my friend. Dwight and I are having a rough time as well, and he does get quite emotional as well. I don't think we will be able to play rook for quite some time-if ever. I feel cheated by God and don't understand why he had to take our friends. First my mother died then Dwight gets Cancer, and now this. Both Dwight and I counted on Al and Rita to be here for us when times get tough for us. I don't understand. I know God has a plan—but to be quite honest—right now I think his plan stinks. But I also know that Albert and Rita are with Jesus and some day we will get to see them again, and just maybe—some good will come from this. Al and Rita would be so pleased if their death brought others to Christ, and their love for Jesus would be shared by others. But in the meantime—Dwight and I are hurting as well as so many of Al and Rita's friends and family. So friends and family, please pray for all of us. Someday I know it won't hurt to smile once again. Just wish it was soon. We are saying our prayers to give comfort to our friend's family and other friends whose hearts are also heavy. Know that you are all in our hearts.

Love,
Rita McGillis"

Journaling was a way for me to connect to the feeling of being near to my family, as best as I could. I tried to put my thoughts into words somehow, so from early on, my newly purchased journal, with a colorful calico cat cover, became my friend and confidant. My original plan was to journal and organize the year coming up while travelling to and from Las Vegas. I had planned to fill the pages with all kinds of priority lists. Now my journaling was to write short entries, basic information about each day, as if I was talking to our boys. I felt it was my duty to write an account of how two down-to-earth adults got so hopelessly lost.

I wrote for family eyes, in case we never saw each other again, not expecting to ever share with others. I wanted them to understand our thinking and be proud of their dad's efforts. Above all, I wanted them to be assured that God's love never left us. I had limited paper to write on. Keeping track of the days and nights helped me feel connected with the world. I knew exactly which date and day of the week I reached. I dared not imagine the days and nights going on without me, instead I purposed in my heart to live my own days and nights as they came, one at a time. I recorded the weather-related details even though the weather pattern hardly changed. It's a very Canadian thing to comment on the weather.

Later, on scraps of paper from the CONEXPO schedule, I wandered into planning menus, thoughts on food and gardening and house remodeling plans, gift ideas for the grandchildren and food again. This was my way of escaping from the harsh reality of my situation which helped me feel not quite so homesick. I would be stranded for just a couple more days, I told myself every day! It was still a head-shaking mystery to me that a series of tiny decisions had led to this dead end!

Being homesick brought back a childhood memory. When I was about four, I got lost in a field of thick grass that was way over my head. I was terrified that a lion was going to catch me and gobble me up. I cried out to Jesus, "Where's my daddy? Help me find him!" Out of nowhere, my dad suddenly appeared and scooped me up in his arms. Even that young, in childlike faith, I knew God had heard my cry. After that, I always expected that the Lord God, who loves me, always would. Now stranded and alone, like a helpless child, I really counted on God hearing my prayers.

If I was a mommy's girl, I didn't set out to be one. I've wondered if I was an overprotected child because of my difficult birth, a forceps delivery. I was told about my mom's difficult recovery. At home I was treated like a porcelain doll, too fragile for hard work or boisterous play with my siblings. I didn't mind that, I got all the easy chores, but sometimes I hated missing out on the fun and excitement. I was the *sissy* and it wouldn't be safe for me to tag along with my brothers on their fishing adventures. The dreaded *sissy* label followed me at school. Partway through elementary school, I made up my mind to get unstuck from it. Even when I didn't feel brave on the inside, from now on I was going to act brave.

My new bravado ways probably confused my classmates. One girl took to badgering me relentlessly until our handsome young teacher, who was the crush of every girl in class, lit into her for being a bully. I sat taller in my desk right up to the moment he turned his attention my way and snapped, "And you, Rita, need to grow up! Quit acting like a sissy!" That dreaded word! I refused to break down in more tears, but seriously, what could have been worse? Looking back, my teacher's strategy worked. It toughened me up. So I was ready when the ringleader of the bully girls cornered and threatened me. I was no match as a fighter, but in a voice as calm as could be I said, "I'm sorry you don't want to be my friend but I would really like to be your friend." She froze for a couple of long seconds then turned on her heels and stomped away! I thought, "Wow, that was a brave thing I just did!" She and I never did become friends, but she never gave me any more trouble. Each test of courage in the next years ahead paid off. Those school day challenges made me grow up and prepare me for even this present time in the wilderness where I was able to believe that God would grant me the courage to face each day and each hour as long as I had breath. In grade three I memorized this verse: *"I can do all things through Christ which strengtheneth me." (Philippians 4:13, KJV)* This verse is often an inspiration for me to this day.

Chapter Eight

Overcoming Fear

Some days when I couldn't contain the flood of sorrows and regrets, I let go and cried my heart out. I soon discovered that the crying didn't help much, but just gave me a headache. I worked even harder at holding myself together. I talked out loud to myself a lot. "Al should have been back by now. He always was a natural-born survivor, blessed with an amazing ability to finish what he started. What if he didn't make it? What if he really did die out there? He is the only one who knows how to find me. No one else even knows where I am." Fear piled on. "What's to become of me out here? I may never be found! If by some miracle I do get rescued, will I be a widow? I'm not ready for this! I don't know how to be a widow! I did not sign up for this!"

I don't know for sure how many days passed before I stopped waiting and watching for Al's return. Everything was just easier when I kept my mind on other things, like what I needed to do next to get through the next hour. Now it was my turn to show courage. I was determined to continue to do everything to survive. I knew I must never give up. Everything I was going to face, Jesus would carry me through. That I had faith in!

I was scared less about dying than I was about what people would say if they found me dead here in no-man's-land. They would surely say, "What possessed these Canadians to come up this way in the first place? In the winter of all things, and without a four-wheel drive! And why didn't that crazy woman just walk out?" I wanted to walk out many times but always changed my mind. I believed it was too cold and dangerous and too far from any shelter. I feared the wild animals. If Al couldn't make it how could I? He would be here by now if he had.

In quiet solitary confinement, I had no choice but to face all my lifelong fears. If I thought they had been tamed long ago, now I found out they were all on pause, just waiting for a chance to roar back to life. All my life my biggest fear was of being alone. Even when I was in crowds I felt alone. I always made sure to stay close to Al who seemed to have no fear. I hated having to go anywhere without him. Now here I was, all by myself.

In these forlorn mountains, I feared the beginning of each day. I woke up afraid of all the things I imagined could or might happen on that day. If I could have, I would have stayed curled up inside my four-wheeled shelter all day. But I had to be brave! I had to do my best. When the daylight began to dim and the darkness started to move in, I had a new battle with fear; as a feeling of dread would come over me. There were few moonlit star-filled night skies. Thankfully, I had three small flashlights, which I used sparingly.

Thoughts like "what if a dangerous stranger came along? Desperate fugitives from the law could find the perfect hideout here. No one would ever find them! If someone wanted to hurt me there was no one to help and nothing I could do to stop them." Feeling vulnerable without Al, I entertained all kinds of nightmarish thoughts. Eventually I realized I should turn those dark thoughts into prayers. Admitting that my fears were exaggerated and possible to overcome by prayer was a breakthrough for me. "Lord, when you send along a rescuer, please make sure it's someone nice. Someone I can trust."

Scary thoughts came and went. "What if I catch a bad cold and what if the cold turns into something worse like bronchitis or pneumonia!" It was a miracle I didn't get seriously sick! Just once I felt a bit feverish with a sore throat that got worse as the day went on. Before settling down for the night I remembered that I had some pure mint extract tablets in my travel bag. I took one good dose, along with my evening fish oil capsule. By morning it was much better.

MOTHER'S DAY MIRACLE

Night-prowling animals were my number one fear. I never saw them but I just knew they were out there in the dark, lurking around, hungry, and waiting. I hoped they would rather eat their usual food and not bother with me. I consoled myself with that thought. I soon realized I would make myself crazy with fear and worry myself to death if I didn't relax and live moment by moment.

One morning, giant paw prints as big as a man's fists circled and recircled the van. My imagined fears turned real. Were the deep impressions in the clay the work of a prowling mountain lion or big cat? I was petrified! I huddled inside for extra-long hours until I couldn't wait any longer. I was out of water and I had to get down to the creek before dark.

I prepared myself for my big exit. I told the Lord, "I'm going out and I'm going to trust you to watch over me." I set off reluctantly, trembling, carefully selecting each step in order to avoid the bulky rocks and mud. Along the way, I encouraged myself by reciting a favourite scripture passage over and over again. *"The Lord is my shepherd; I shall not want. He maketh me to lie down in green pastures: he leadeth me beside the still waters. He restoreth my soul: he leadeth me in the paths of righteousness for his name's sake. Yea, though I walk through the valley of the shadow of death, I will fear no evil: for thou art with me; thy rod and thy staff they comfort me." (Psalm 23:1–3, KJV)* Those words had a powerful calming effect but I still looked around and over my shoulder as I picked my way down the steep bank to the creek. I wondered if I was being stalked. Leaning down to dip and fill each water bottle was always a slow process but this day it seemed to take an eternity. Wild hungry eyes were watching me. I knew it! The hair on the back of my neck stood up. I peered along the edges of the banks, first on one side and then the other. At any moment, I expected to lock eyes with the big cat that was sizing me up as easy prey.

Suddenly, like turning to a different channel, a familiar Bible story dropped into my mind. Just like me, the Samaritan woman walked out of her safe village alone to draw water from a well. Just like me, she was lonely and rejected (I felt forgotten) but Jesus befriended her and struck up a conversation. He knew all about her. It surprised her that Jesus cared about her and promised that he could give her living water and she would never thirst again (found in the *Bible* in John 4:14). Jesus knew all about my troubles too. I was taken up with this story and forgot about my fears. The beautiful song that commemorates her story, "Fill my cup, Lord" by Richard Blanchard (1959), came to mind. I began to hum the melody. Like a flash flood, I was filled with joy in place of fear. I forgot about the big cat. I hummed the song all the way back to my home on wheels, feeling free as my little bird, who came alongside and fluttered with me back up the hill.

Later that day, I followed the paw prints and saw that the big cat had walked right past the van. It was clear that the cat went on the path way off into the hills. My imagination was the problem. Another lesson learned. I saw the remains of a dear carcass on the way. The cat was fed. I thanked the Lord for his protection. The Lord has been with me so far so why should I doubt? Watching and waiting and looking above, I was beginning to have more joy than fear. That's hard to express in words. All I know is; the days grew longer, the fears faded and the times were precious. Those precious memories of growing in faith and courage have not left me to this day.

After a few hours reclining in the front seat each afternoon, reading or napping, I felt rather stiff. At night my only other option was to stretch out on the back bench seat, so I alternated my routine during the long dark nights. When the inevitable darkness moved in at the end of a day, I sometimes lightened my burden with a little humor. "Okay, Rita, which hotel would you like to stay in tonight? Would you prefer the lovely reclining passenger seat, or the luxurious miniature bench seat? It felt good to act silly. What a relief. It was a good thing that I felt quite okay with laughing at myself. I was sorry no one else was around to laugh with me. It felt so good to hear the sound of someone laughing even if it was just my own voice. Laughter really is the best medicine!

How silly I must have looked doing my impersonation of a mouse catcher. In my mind, a wild mouse chase offered my best and only hope for a meal. No one saw me scampering to and fro across the scruffy fields, without the remotest chance on earth of capturing a furry scurrying little critter, without the slightest idea what I would do if I ever actually caught one. I had planned to eat it but it would have been a catch and release I'm sure!

I was really hungry but not too weak yet to try another idea. My next hunter-gatherer plan was to go looking for grouse eggs in nests they had constructed in dense bushy areas on the ground. My search efforts were once again in vain. I guess it was too early for grouse nesting season. Maybe my plan was short-sighted. Even if I had found eggs in a nest, I'm not sure if I could have handled eating them fresh from the shell, though it would have been better than eating a raw mouse!

Meanwhile, nature continued to call as the days went by. The holes that Al had prepared for me were all used up. Now I had to find a new area to dig more holes. The only place that offered convenience, because of the wet mud, was the sloped ground right behind the van. Privacy and dignity was still an important consideration in my mind, so I dug a row of small holes another level up, on a steeper grade. I cautioned myself to be extra careful to keep my balance. I could just see myself tumbling down one of these times. Sure enough, with my pants down around my ankles, I lost my balance and tumbled slowly down the rocky muddy bank. "Help me, Jesus!" I landed awkwardly at the foothill. The rolling descent didn't hurt me physically, although I could have easily had cuts and scrapes. It just utterly embarrassed me. My first instinct was to quickly grab a hold of my pants and pull them up. I quickly checked all around to make sure there was no one around who had witnessed my fall. I laughed at such a reaction. Isn't that exactly what I wanted…someone around? Wasn't that my only hope…that someone would come along and find me here!

Lightheartedness was replacing my fears. I laughed in my sleep several times and woke myself up. My dreams were vivid, like I was watching a movie. One dream was about one of my daughters-in-law being pregnant and having twins. It seemed hilarious to me at the time. Another was about my youngest son Carl chauffeuring his cousins from Terrace, in a mini bus, all over Penticton to see the tourist sights after picking them up from the airport. Only thing is, they were late for our funeral because of it. You've got to know Carl—he sure can get carried away talking and being the comedian! That was my entertainment for the night!

The ultimate dream was about a handsome cowboy who spotted me out here and lifted me onto his horse and brought me to safety. That idea was on my mind because earlier that day, I had seen and heard in the far distance what looked like someone on a horse and a dog walking along side. I heard the winnowing of the horse and the barking of the dog. I called out as loud as I could and honked the horn, but to no avail. It was so far away! I was so sad they could not see me or maybe ignored me because they would have no idea I was stranded. Perhaps I was just imagining things because I wanted so much to be rescued! Silly as that was, I met a very special cowboy four years later.

Chapter Nine

Forty Days

I imagined the worst case scenario. What if rescuers came by when I was at the creek or exploring, out of sight of the van for even a few minutes? If someone came this far, I would hope that they would notice me. Wouldn't that be Murphy's Law! To be on the safe side, I made signs to post on the front window. Then I made more signs, each one telling a part of our sad story. With wax crayons I had stashed away in my glove box for my grandchildren, I scrawled "mayday" messages. I included details: our names, where we were from, our phone number, our eldest son Raymond's name and number and the date we were expected back home. I also posted our GPS coordinates and noted we had no mobile phone connection. I put up my makeshift messages on the van windows on every side and stepped back to survey my handiwork.

In case a rancher came out only as far as the cattle gate, I made one more "HELP, I'm lost!" sign with my plea for help. I stashed it inside a shiny green shopping bag, zipped it up, walked out to the cattle guard and tied it to the gate. The next time I went to check it wasn't there. It had blown away. No matter how tightly I fastened that green bag, the wind blew it off. I got so frustrated at trying to find it in the scrub grass so, I gave up and quit bothering with it at all. I found another use for the green zipped bag, to carry my water bottles. Each day it was getting increasingly harder to carry six water bottles back up from the creek. I waited in hope that someone, someday, would come out this far and see my signs. That wasn't going to happen until the mud dried up and the mud was worse now than on the day we got stuck. No one would come here on purpose. They would have to be as lost as I was. I gradually kept adding to my signs as I thought of more helpful information just in case I died before anyone came out here.

When I woke up to the fortieth day I wondered about why I was still here. Even more amazing to me was that I was still alive! I was weak and burdened with my routine. I decided to take another walk to the top of the hill behind my van while I was still barely able to. I wanted to try to build a fire one more time. I was tired of waiting for someone to show up. I needed to find a way to attract attention! I had to give it my best shot! It was a nice sunny day and warmer than usual. Maybe today would be the day! I brought some crumpled phone book pages, my magnifying glass and gathered some twigs, setting it all up in a dead clump of scrub brush. I captured the sunlight quickly with the magnifying glass and it ignited successfully! I blew gently to encourage the little flame to grow. My short moment of triumph ended when my feathered friend landed smack in the middle of the bush and the fire snuffed out in a flash as if I had poured water over it. "Oh no, why is she doing this?" I instantly remembered the burning bush story from the Bible. I laid myself out on the ground and cried out to the Lord, "Help me Lord." I felt like I was on holy ground. I realized my life was still in His hands. God's sweet presence wrapped around me like a warm comforter, a feeling that I did not want to let go of.

I got up slowly and looked around over the hills. What a view! This moment reminded me of the time when Jesus was fasting for forty days and nights and was subsequently brought to the wilderness and tempted by Satan. This story is in the Bible in Matthew 4: 1–11. Satan wanted to have Jesus hand over the Kingdom to him. I wondered why I was still out here after forty days, hungry, weak and discouraged. I was tempted to give up but I really did not want to die. I would rather go home to Penticton! I was thinking out loud so I said to Jesus, "This is crazy! I am just a mere human! You can't expect me to live more than forty days without a meal. You are the

Son of God! Your Word says you were very hungry and weak after forty days in the wilderness. Without your help I will not live much longer!" So I yelled out loud, "Get behind me Satan!" It worked for Jesus so why not. Then I yelled out again, with more expression, like I really meant it! "Get behind me Satan!"

    I stared in silence for a while. Nothing visible happened but slowly, a wonderful wave of peace came over me. Mere words cannot describe this peace. Light and warmth embraced me, my inner fight dissolved. Gentle waves of peace washed over my soul. I found freedom on a higher plain! I raised my voice in song, giving thanks and praise to God. I could not control my circumstances but I could control what was within me! Everything felt different now after that mountain top experience. Though I still hoped to go home, maybe God had different plans. I had become okay with that. It took the weight off my shoulders to simply rest and let God look after things. Slowly I returned to my van and tidied up and repacked my clothes, separating mine from Al's. I put a few things in the smallest travel bag as if I was waiting for a ride at any moment even though I did not know if I had more time to live. Perhaps I would not wake up tomorrow or perhaps God would send someone to me. That evening I settled into reading the Psalms for comfort. *"I sought the Lord, and he heard me, and delivered me from all my fears." (Psalm 34:4, KJV) "I waited patiently for the LORD; and he inclined unto me, and heard my cry. He brought me up also out of an horrible pit, out of the miry clay, and set my feet upon a rock, and established my goings. And he hath put a new song in my mouth, even praise unto our God: many will see it, and fear, and shall trust in the LORD." (Psalm 40:1–3, KJV)*

Chapter Ten

Hearing My Voice

I found that reading was consoling to my soul. The books I brought for our trip were very welcomed; to draw myself into another thinking zone away from my troubles and to give me hope for days ahead. My family tradition was that soul food comes before tackling the day. It was natural for me to keep that tradition up in the mountains. My body was under-nourished to the point of starvation but my soul was fat! Morning after lonely morning, I savoured the "Our Daily Bread" devotional book and the Bible throughout the day. I started with Genesis, then continued through Exodus and kept on going. I saved the Psalms for dessert in the evening light.

The two books I had stowed away for our Las Vegas time were my soul food supplement! The strange thing about those books was, they happened to be a good topic to read about in my present circumstance. The titles were "How to Live Your Full Potential for God" and the other one was "One Heartbeat Away: Your Journey into Eternity." These were books Al had just finished reading which he suggested to bring on our trip in case I got bored at the equipment show. I liked the sound of living my full potential better, so I read it first. The other, I read second because I was curious. Maybe I needed to know more about dying, just in case!

"One Heartbeat Away: Your Journey into Eternity" by Mark Cahill, an American basketball star. He wrote about the real-life courage it takes to do your best, win or lose, not just on a basketball court, but at every life challenge. He posed two great questions: "What awaits you after your final breath?" and "What do you know for sure?" I pondered those questions in light of the real possibility that I might be close to my final breath. I wondered if Al was already home free. Something I knew for sure was that he was safe with Jesus, wherever he was.

"How to Reach Your Full Potential for God" by Charles Stanley, seemed right for me at this crucial time and I wanted to apply every key principle and turn each one into a personal goal. "Never settle for less than wanting God's best. Be ready to do the work that it takes. Keep a clean heart. Keep a clear mind. Use your gifts. Keep a healthy body. Keep right relationships. Keep a balanced schedule and set aside unstructured time. Take only God-approved risks and go down paths He asks you to walk."

I had the luxury of time to let the words and thoughts sink in deep. I was amazed at how brilliantly the books described life here on earth and in heaven. With the help of two brave authors who dug deep to share their life experiences, I didn't ever get into complete hopelessness or despair even though at times, I felt lonely and sad, and I was physically weak and anxious to go home. After I read both books from cover to cover, I started at page one all over again! Nothing I read, good as it was, shed as much light or gave as much strength as my Bible did. The words of scripture came to life and leapt off the pages. The words were food for my soul, my daily bread. Heaven worked its way into my world with the turn of each page from Al's personal Bible that still bore his finger prints. With him in mind, I imagined what we would say to each other in response.

In my reading room on wheels, I alternated front and back and left and right seats to catch the sunrays on the few sunny days. I read and napped and read some more and curled up with my blankets, often past the sunset. To hear my own voice and thinking was much like a conversation that stopped momentarily and picked-up spontaneously throughout the day. That's what I call "praying without ceasing." I often felt like Jesus was right there responding to my words inspiring me to wait patiently. One day, I recall leaning toward the seat next to me to face Him, forgetting for a moment that I could not see or touch Jesus. I knew His presence was real!

This talking and praying out loud to the lord reminded me of Al, who was so strong in his faith. He talked with Jesus like He was right there with him all the time. I practiced Al's conversational style. Standing alone and lifting my little voice to the starlit sky felt awkward at first but little by little, carrying on a friendly relaxed dialogue with my Heavenly Father became as natural as breathing. It was a comfort to hear a human voice, even if it was just my own. I asked the Lord many questions and waited for His gentle answers that came to me in my thoughts. Words can't begin to do justice to the great comfort of the *Voice of Love* talking back to my lonely heart through my thoughts and prayers.

Chapter Eleven

Homeward Bound

The forty-eighth day of my lonely days was the most lovely weather day so far. I noticed that my little feathered friend was not there or maybe I forgot about her because I was feeling kind of dreamy, sleeping my morning away. At about noon when the sun was so warm and lovely, I finally got up and out. I needed water so I went for a dreaded walk to get some. I really wondered how many more days I would have the strength to do this. The walk was slow and difficult. I sure wished I could shed my layers and lay in the water, but no. Wouldn't it be my lucky day that someone would appear just then! I rested quite a while at my water ditch before climbing back up the slope. I took it very slowly, singing along the way to cheer myself up.

As I walked, I was thinking about my friend Rita M. "It is her birthday today!" I felt so bad that I was not there to have a party for her and our friends! I prayed for her again and hoped she was okay.

I still had a strong desire to have a sponge bath by the time I got back. I debated whether I should use my water for this. Yes, I should! It was the warmest day yet and a good one to enjoy a freshening up for sure. It was so warm outside that I was able to wash my hair and then blow dry it in the wind. This time, I parted my hair and braided it to take the pressure off of my sore neck. What a pleasure to feel the warmth of the sun and only needing one layer of clothes on under my lighter jacket.

I went for a little *slow as a turtle* stroll just in front of my van on the trail, pacing back and forth, feeling a comforting presence of the Lord with me. On this afternoon the clouds parted and the sun came out to stay a while. I looked at the meadow over across the way. What I saw next was so magnificent. This earthly plot of ground transformed into a piece of heaven, sparkling with countless little mountain bluebirds just like my personal feathered friend, dancing and singing like a host of tiny angels. I gazed in wonder and awe. Was I dreaming? Beams of sunlight shone through the opening in the clouds in a light show of rainbow colors. I wondered if this was a glimpse of heaven. If I walked into it would I be beamed up? It was a lovely thought! The beauty declared the glory of God to me. I dared not move. I did not want this to go away. I let my heart drink in the beauty of the scene. "Just in case you are listening Lord," I whispered, "I am still here. This would be the perfect meadow for a helicopter to land in to rescue me. It's not too late." Just a moment later, I said, "I'm sorry! Forgive me for telling you what to do, but you have to agree it is a good idea, right?" The light show lasted only a short while longer. The birds flew away to other meadows. The sun moved along and the light faded to earth-toned shadows.

I had to rest after this. My strength was failing. This experience changed something in me. I moved closer to the light (Jesus). I thought more about heaven, realizing my time was short. I was exhausted from my exciting day. "I think I'm going to die out here." I was mumbling to myself, "So I'm going to get ready." I felt excited, like a child getting ready to go home after a long time away. I could hardly wait but I fell asleep well before dark before I could do anything about it.

The morning came quickly. It was the forty-ninth day since we had left Penticton! It was Friday, May 6th. I was surprised to still be alive. I wondered about my poor mother! She must be beside herself wondering where we are! Maybe she has died of a heart attack from the grief and stress. Oh, and my children! What could they be thinking by now? I wished so much that I could be home for Mother's Day! In biblical terms numbers have significant meaning. "Seven" represents completion and wholeness. But seven times seven holds even richer symbolism. "Forty-nine" conveys perfect peace—paid in full—Shalom.

This Friday of Mother's Day weekend was the brightest and sunniest of all the days since we first set out for our trip to Nevada, seven weeks earlier. I woke up on that sunny morning with a sense that something big was going to happen. I felt I had reached the end of one thing and the beginning of another. What a strange feeling! My bird friend was not there to greet me that morning.

If this was my time to die then I had to finish getting ready first. The prospect of being beamed up to heaven now seemed to be good timing and a good way to finish my years on earth. For many days, I had noticed that I was sleeping more and drinking less. The less I drank the less energy I had to stay awake. It became a major chore to refill my water bottles. The trip to the creek and back would drain my little store of strength, but my water bottles were almost empty, used for shampooing my hair and taking a sponge bath the day before. Now I only had half a bottle of water left. As long as I was able, I needed to get water.

The trip to the creek today, I felt, would be my last. I got started, one step at a time, with a couple of the empty bottles. I felt dizzy and nauseous. My heart hurt with every beat and my lungs burned with every breath. By now I was wishing I had not started. I made progress in slow motion, stopping every couple of steps to recover. Soon I was very short of breath. I was worried that the chest pain may be a heart attack coming on. No way did I want to drop dead out here in the open where animals could feed on me! At the creek bed, I bent down to dip the bottles and slowly sipped on water hoping to gather a little strength to get back. My full bottles were too heavy to carry back. Like I had the day before, I tethered them to my vinyl shopping bag with my belt and dragged them behind me along the trail. I put one foot in front of the other for as far as I could but my legs were caving. Dropping to my hands and knees I slowly crawled uphill to the van. I prayed out loud, "Oh, Lord, help me get back to shelter!" It took all the strength I could muster to open the van side door. I collapsed onto the threshhold to rest and catch my breath. "Thank you, Lord!"

I knew it was time to let go. I didn't feel at all afraid but felt instead a strange mix of joy and sorrow. The worst part was imagining how hard it was going to be for our sons and grandchildren to lose both of us, especially because of the strange way it all happened. The best part was the sweet feeling that I was ready to go to my forever home. I made my journal entry as positive as possible, under the circumstances. Then I got myself cleaned up, combing and re-braiding my hair. The finishing touch was to put on the pair of new white socks that I had set aside and saved for the equipment show. Now I would wear these white socks for my own quiet funeral and the van would be my humble tomb. Satisfied that all my affairs were in order, I opened the side window flaps to let fresh breezes flow through, then tucked my pillow under my head, wrapped my blanket around me, and stretched out on the back bench seat. I closed my eyes, took a deep breath and recited the famous children's bedtime prayer. "Now I lay me down to sleep. I pray the Lord my soul to keep. If I should die before I wake, I pray the Lord my soul to take." Quite content with that, with my eyes still closed, I crossed my arms the way arms are placed in a casket. "Beam me up, Lord," I said before willing myself to drift off on my way into heaven. In full expectation, I fell into a lovely sleep.

Chapter Twelve

The Great Rescue

But that's not the way things went. After a short sleep, I was suddenly aware of a distant noise. In my foggy thoughts, I recognized it as a familiar sound. "Could it be ATVs?" I found myself standing at my open side van door waving frantically although I don't remember opening the door. There came a young couple whizzing right past me. "Why are they not stopping? Can't they see me?" Then, the next person came around the corner. He slowed down to have a good look at me. I leaned out and waved hard, beckoning him to come, yelling "Help, Help!" He stopped and cautiously approached me while waving at the others, who had already noticed his move towards me. They appeared unsure that this was a good idea! I was so relieved and promptly slumped to the floor with weakness. I really wondered if this was for real or if was I dreaming?

"What are you doing here, ma'am?" he said, with great bewilderment. With tears I answered, "I'm just a dumb Canadian who got lost." I told them how long I had waited for help to come and that we had been stranded since March 19 and how Al walked out towards Mountain City for help but did not return. At first they could hardly believe my story. I shook my finger at them and I showed them my diary to prove to them my sad predicament. They were moved to tears. The three of them, all members of the same family, soon realized that I needed immediate medical attention and promptly went for help, promising to come back as soon as they could. Before they left, they gave me some bottled water and snacks. I sure enjoyed the clean water, but I could not swallow the nacho chips or the beef jerky. I had no appetite, my tongue was sore and I felt nauseous and dizzy!

I sat there for some time, dumbfounded and enjoying tiny sips of clean water. I wondered why now! I was ready to die! By now I had concluded that death was better than going home without Albert. I had a serious conversation in my mind with God about that. I sensed He was saying, "Trust Me. Albert is not your concern now! I want you to go home and be a witness of the love and mercy that I have shown you." I was thinking, "Are you talking to me? Me, tell everyone? I'm really shy!" But somehow I knew God was serious. He was challenging me. Was I willing or did God have to find someone else to be my mouth piece? I instantly recalled the story of Moses and Aaron from the Bible. The story is in Exodus 4. God chose Aaron to speak instead of Moses, who felt he was not a speaker. I knew I had to answer now! In my heart I said, "Yes Lord, with your help. You know I am not good with words." I felt a confirmation that God heard my answer when I immediately felt a surge of heat go through my body from the top of my head to the soles of my feet. What a feeling! It was like a huge adrenalin rush.

While my rescuers were getting help I slowly repacked my little travel bag and tidied up the van a little and freshened myself up some more. I hadn't looked in the mirror for weeks. I pulled some chin hairs and combed my braided hair. I hardly looked like the person I was before. I was so excited! I sat and waited while help was on the way, thankful for this time alone to think about my unexpected survival at this critical moment. Not being rushed away from the Wilderness when they first arrived was probably a good thing. I had a couple hours to let it sink in. "I am going to survive and I will see my family soon!" Just to think that this might not have happened that day if this family had not gone out on this spring day to scout for shed Elk antlers and if they would not have wandered off in a direction that they had not planned on. They had found one antler and were intent on finding the mate to it. Instead, they came upon a stranded Canadian woman. God knew what he was doing. Truly a miracle!

In just a few hours the rescue helicopter landed exactly where I thought it should, in the lovely meadow where I saw the beautiful bird show just the day before. I was ready with my small suitcase in hand. There they were, Troy, Chad, and Whitney jumping off their ATVs after guiding in the rescue team to me. Soon we shared hugs and I thanked them for their kindness. They left me as the medical team took over from there. I did not hesitate to say that Jesus was with me when they asked how I hung on to hope. I was a big whirl of emotions, yet my body was so weak. My mouth was speaking words of thanks and praise to God freely like I have never done before. The two medics were very compassionate and gentle with me. They cautioned me to try and relax while taking my vitals and they asked me many questions. They talked to the doctor via satellite phone while reading parts of my diary about my eating routine. They were very aware that they just witnessed a real miracle. Soon we were in the air on the way to the hospital. My family was notified of my rescue very quickly.

Our friend Dwight was alone at home when our eldest son Raymond's call came in. He got a kick out of relaying the good report to our circle of praying friends. "I've got news for you," he started out every call. "Are you sitting down?" On the day after the worst birthday of her life, Rita M came home to her best day. After hearing Dwight's good news, she says, she smiled so much she strained her cheek muscles. At 11:43 p.m. Rita M composed another heartfelt email, sent out on May 6, 2011.

> "Dear friends and family,
>
> It is now late at night and I am ready for bed. So tired, but had to tell all of you that my "best-est" friend Rita Chretien has been found ALIVE. What a miracle! After forty-nine days living only on water and a small amount of food she is now probably about thirty pounds lighter. Her families are on their way to Twin Falls hospital right now. What a wonderful Mother's Day gift they

received. Rita was found the day after my birthday. What a wonderful gift I received. So thank you one and all for your prayers, God does listen and sometimes he grants miracles. Now please continue to pray that Albert will be found. We already know what prayer can do, so come on everyone, we did it once, let's do it again. Love you all and saying my prayers and thanks tonight.

Rita McGillis"

Family and friends rejoiced and praised God for answered prayer. My rescue news was broken dramatically to my sister Ingrid. She was at the REM Lee Theatre in Terrace, BC on Friday evening while watching a performance by the local Christian school. She noticed our sister-in-law Shannon, married to our brother Richard, running up and down the aisles, searching frantically. She was looking for Ingrid, to tell her the miracle news. Ingrid had never given up hope that I would be found alive. It was a joyous time to be sure, but tempered because Al was not found with me.

Throughout our mysterious disappearance, my brother Dave and his wife Renie had supported and encouraged our distraught mother. They put their lives on hold for all those weeks of silence. They never knew when they were going to hear something, so they were always waiting, wondering if we were killed by wild animals or at the hands of some violent person. At first, Dave thought the best but after several weeks he felt the disappearance was just too long. Renie never gave up hope. She kept on thinking of different things that could have happened. She challenged Dave's conclusion that there was no way we could still be alive. Even so, they are people of faith and never stopped praying. Dave was at work in his shop at their lakeside home in northern BC when he picked up the call from our mother. "They found Rita" was all she got out before she burst into sobs. Dave waited quietly on his end of the line, giving her time to grieve the loss of a second child, her youngest daughter. As her crying slowed down she was able to relay the rest of the news: "She's alive!" Dave could literally not take in what his ears had just heard. The words sank in slowly. It was a sweet moment all right, but again, it left a bittersweet aftertaste because Al was not found with me.

Chapter Thirteen

The Royal Treatment

After a twenty-minute flight to the St. Luke's Magic Valley Regional Medical Center in Twin Falls, Idaho, I was warmly welcomed with quite a fan fair! I soon heard the headlines and news about us from the nurse. Really—I was so embarrassed! What trouble we caused! The nurse brought me some delicious hot chicken broth and a few soda crackers. Oh how lovely to finally enjoy a hot drink and some real food! I was just about to have some more but the doctor walked in and grabbed my crackers and threw them in the garbage! He said that I should not have had that. After meeting my doctor and being checked over, in a very solemn voice, he explained the danger of eating normal food so soon after starvation and that we needed to take it slowly and carefully in the days ahead. I had to be fed intravenously for a few days. He seemed stressed that I was in serious condition!

For the life of me, I couldn't stop smiling as this kind doctor informed me that my stomach had shrunk to the approximate size of a walnut. I wasn't just thirty pounds lighter—I was critically dehydrated and in danger of internal organs shutting down completely! I tried my best to absorb the gravity of my condition. The loss of trace minerals may have affected all organs, including my heart, kidneys and brain. I believed him because everything hurt, even my eyes. My tongue was white and sore. Even so, nothing he said worried me. I had just been healed by waves of pure love. My joy banks overflowed and I couldn't hold them back. I was in la-la land, hardly concerned about my condition. I just wanted to close my eyes and go to sleep!

To avoid "Re-eating Syndrome," a serious post-starvation condition in its own right, foods had to be slowly introduced. First, I had intravenous feedings to restore depleted minerals such as potassium. I also had to drink a liquid medicine that tasted like metal. It was good that the murky water I had collected from the shallow ditch was icy cold, as that likely helped prevent dangerous microorganisms and parasites while allowing me to ingest some of the valuable minerals. The doctor was happy to know that I had taken fish oil every day, which surely was another great help in my survival for so long. More amazing was my rescue in the *nick of time!* I know I couldn't have lasted much longer—possibly just a few more hours.

I soon had the long awaited phone call to my family. What a joy to hear my son Raymond's voice! Our emotions soared! He could hardly believe it was my voice he was hearing and that I was alive. I assured him I would be okay. He said he was coming to see me the next day! What joy to hear that!

Soon after my admittance to the emergency ward, I was settled into a warm motion air bed that seemed like floating on a cloud and then hooked up to an IV. The doctors were very concerned about my fragile condition. I was in starvation mode. They were so careful and kind to me. They fussed over me like I was very delicate. I certainly got the royal treatment while I was in their excellent care at St. Luke's.

The rescue report spread like wildfire beyond just our family and friends thanks in large part to the internet and media interest. An online search for Albert and Rita Chretien still turns up 20 million plus hits! Headlines blared: "Survivor! As in real life—not reality TV"—to, "I'm just blown away by your strength!" On the site Missing Persons of America: "I could not believe this when I saw it. Rita Chretien has been found alive!" On a national missing persons site: "Unbelievably, Rita Chretien, who has been missing since March 19, was found stranded on a remote logging road in Elko County, Nevada had survived on only water over the last seven weeks. Without communication and the conditions being as harsh as they have been, it's all pretty miraculous!" A survival expert weighed in on a news station: "The fact that she's alive now—I was dumbfounded when I heard the news, just blown away. It's very unusual to have anyone survive that long, especially by yourself in an environment like that." As the news traveled far and wide on that entry into Mother's Day weekend, I rested, warm and worry-free, in intensive care luxury better than a five-star resort.

Early Saturday morning, Dwight and Rita McGillis reached me by phone. In overjoyed shock Rita reacted to my hello. "It's really your voice. It's real!" My mother was next, what a joy to hear her voice! She was in a hospital too! From one hospital bed over 2,000 kilometers away to another we expressed our love for each other. I was relieved to hear she was still alive.

Before calling it a day, and a most magnificent day at that, I entered a short note in my journal. My block letter printing days were over and done with. I switched back to normal cursive writing style that was here to stay. "May 7: I'm doing better, getting my strength back and lots of blood tests and medications. They are all so great, a bouquet of flowers already from X-ray dept."

Many more flowers found their way to my room. I had to look and then sent them away to another area of the hospital because they were not allowed in the intensive care unit.

The next morning, I requested a visit from the pastor of the Church of the Nazarene in Twin Falls. Later that same day, Pastor Steve Myers arrived to offer a powerful prayer of comfort and encouragement. He had chosen one Scripture reading in advance of his visit. It happened to be Psalm 86, one of my anchor passages that I read several times out in my van. *"Bow down thine ear, O Lord, hear me: for I am poor and needy. Preserve my soul; for I am holy: O thou my God, save thy servant that trusteth in thee. be merciful unto me, O Lord: for I cry unto thee daily." (Psalm 86:1–3, KJV)* We had a very pleasant visit. The pastor graciously stepped outside while my family arrived, so we could have our long-awaited reunion and hugs.

After a thirteen-hour beeline drive from Penticton to Twin Falls, Raymond and his wife Jennifer along with Albert's oldest brother Henry and his wife Betty, walked into my hospital room. What a joyous moment! Afraid for weeks that I'd never see them again, I hugged them all, not wanting to let go! They had braced themselves for finding me in terrible shape. It baffled them to see me looking not just fine, but great! I wasn't well, but I looked good because of the joyful radiance on my face. How awesome that moment was! What an encouragement to see them and hear their voices and to receive their loving hugs! Pastor Steve came back in the room when we were ready for prayer. He briefly met my family and then he encouraged us with the same reading of scripture from Psalm 86. He also prayed for us and then kindly left us to continue our precious reunion. What a fine man of God! Later he came back again to say goodbye before I went home to Penticton.

My husband's three sisters with their spouses from Washington and from British Columbia, also arrived that second evening. My son Dale flew in from Alberta the next day and my son Carl stayed home in Penticton to look after our business. Carl and I had a consoling visit on the phone instead. They were all amazed that I had survived. How precious to see and hear them all! I was just so happy to be alive!

The morning after the family arrived, I had a long awaited hot shower, my first in fifty days! With saran-wrapped IV paraphernalia, I sat in the hot shower for quite some time to soak in the awesome pleasure of the moment. My thick, long hair was tangled and matted. My neck was weak and sore from the weight of it. I more or less commanded the nurse to cut off my pony tail after I was settled back in bed. She said, "No, I better not." Then I playfully shouted, "Cut it now. I'm a crazy woman!" Well, we laughed so hard that another nurse came running to see what was going on! My heart monitor was dinging out of control as we continued to laugh. What a relief! My hair felt light and looked lovely after she blow dried it for me. I sure enjoyed all the pampering. When Raymond and Jennifer came by that morning shortly after the hair episode they were surprised. I looked much better than the night before and I am sure I smelled better too!

Raymond and Jennifer filled me in on the drama at home and at the business. They also told me about the global media coverage and used their laptop computer to show me all of the "Mother's Day Miracle" headlines and other news stories I had missed. I felt bad that we had caused so much trouble!

Dale had good news from home for me. He shared with me how his sons, Isaac and Joshua, had been through quite a stretch in faith through this whole ordeal. They both came to him and wanted to accept Jesus as Saviour and Lord. What good news for me to hear! All of my grandchildren were excited that grandma was alive!

With the plethora of news reporters camped out across from the hospital Raymond, along with a doctor, prepared to say a few words on behalf of the family and report on my condition, at a press conference that day. I wished pastor Neil from my home church could be here with us to pray. I'm sure he did too! Right then we had a surprise phone call from him—a "God moment"—right when family members who had arrived were gathered around my hospital bed holding hands and about to pray. We were all so excited! I talked to him on speaker phone so all of us could hear. He could hardly talk at first. He was so emotional. He prayed for all of us, a precious moment that I will never forget.

The media throng gathered at the first St. Luke's news conference on that Sunday for their "Mother's Day Angle." The Chretien family had their mother back and they waited to hear the reaction. Jennifer sat by Raymond and held his hand throughout the major news conference. Still in a state of wonder and awe, Raymond read a prepared statement and answered questions from the assembled media: "We were praying for a miracle and boy did we get one! We're stunned. We haven't fully digested it. This is the biggest miracle we could ever ask for! Our mom had a very clear indication there would be something on Friday, whether it was to go home to be with her Saviour or be rescued. And it was to be rescued! What the doctors said about her only having a couple of days—she was feeling that as well. It could have been any moment. If the rescuers hadn't shown up she wouldn't have made it." "I think," he said, "a lot of it was mental preparation, just getting to that point and being at peace about it either way. She's a Christian and she reads her Bible every day. She had books and she had time to think and pray and just prepare for whichever outcome was going to come. She didn't know what it was but she was prepared." From a survivor standpoint, he said, his mom had made a lot of right choices. He told how I rationed the small amount of trail mix, making it stretch for a week by eating just a tablespoon a day. When the trail mix ran out my daily diet included morning and evening fish oil capsules, one or two hard candies and snow-melt or water from a run-off creek. Pressed to describe how he felt seeing his mother again he said, "Mom is an amazing person. She is a giving person. It's so hard to find words to describe her in the way I feel about her. She is genuine. She cares about people. I don't know what to say. She is just amazing! I would have hardly known anything had happened to her. It's just her, just the way I remember." Lost for more words, he repeated, "It's amazing!"

The inevitable question was asked: "Just how did your parents end up on that remote forestry service road?" Raymond gave an unvarnished answer: "It is our understanding they took a few wrong turns. They wanted to take a scenic route and they ended up on a road that the map led them to believe, rightly or wrongly, was a much safer road than it was. I don't believe they were prepared for winter weather. They don't go camping."

They asked about our first phone conversation. Raymond shared about how sorry I was for all the trouble the family went through. "She felt extremely bad for us all. She was extremely apologetic." He gave credit where it was due. "What really kept our mother alive," he said again, "was her faith, that and her refusal to give up."

They asked if the family planned to set up a trust fund to accept financial support. He answered without hesitating: "No. We don't want to make this about money." He concluded with a take-home lesson: "Never give up. Never lose your faith. Miracles happen. Never underestimate that." He shifted the focus. "There's still one more to come in and we are praying for another miracle. The search continues for our father."

The attending physician at that first media conference emphasized how extremely rare it was for a person to live after going so long without food. It is very unusual for a person to have survived this type of ordeal, let alone be doing this well. He confirmed that I might have died within a day or two, maybe less. He attributed my success partly to my good health before we were marooned, partly to remaining calm and partly to keeping myself in good spirits. He said, "she obviously had the mind-set of survival. That must have been something which helped her go as long as she had. Not giving up is the most important thing and everything else has to stem from that."

Over the next few days, us girls had a special time of reminiscing about their brother Albert and all his antics growing up. We had a lot of tears of joy and sorrows. It was a long time since we had a visit all together. My four brothers-in-law and my son Dale went out on a day trip to have a look at the stranded van. They had a great time together out there reminiscing about Albert as they were travelling. Even though the guys met up with the people who were storing the van, they could not retrieve it until the roads improved. I was not so sure that I wanted it back. I suggested that Henry blow it up! He talked me into keeping it for the time being and deciding later, after I get it home again. A few weeks later Henry and an employee from our business went back to get it from Mountain Home where it had been hauled to—a compound for safe keeping. I drove the van as my main vehicle until very recently because of the sentimental value.

Family came to witness the miracle of my survival and to wait for word on Albert. I was questioned in great detail by a detective and then the Sheriff before they went out to search. The next few days were sobering, realizing that this was likely a recovery operation. We continued to pray for another miracle. I was disappointed and surprised that his remains were not found that week.

I never imagined how enjoyable it could be to eat a bit of Jell-O. After a few days I enjoyed my first tiny meal of fish, rice and green beans (as reported on the news) and it tasted like a feast. The next day I ate a small breakfast wrap and a fresh garden salad. That tasted heavenly! I asked for a repeat the following day. On my last morning there, I savoured my first hot cup of flavored coffee in celebration of one of the nurse's birthday. Wow, the flavors seemed so vivid!

With much help from the hospital's social worker, Raymond and Jennifer took care of the medical travel insurance details. What a relief that our insurance company would cover all of my hospital expenses and my medical flight home to Canada. Although I wanted to stay longer to continue my recovery, after four nights in St. Luke's wonderful care, the insurer was very anxious to get me back to Penticton, British Columbia. It seemed I was a patient at St. Luke's for much longer than five days because I experienced so many precious moments. The Spirit of God was in that place for sure! I will never forget the doctors and nurses who were so kind.

I did not want to leave without knowing where my husband Al was but I had no choice. I was emotionally worn out! Daily events were moving along too quickly to fully embrace. The nurses and doctors gave me a sweet farewell (more on this in a moment). Staff and family made a plan to stay longer and celebrate the birthday of one of my special nurses. The reporters from the various news outlets relaxed over that afternoon, not knowing that I would be on my way home soon. My few belongings were all packed and I was ready for the flight home with my son Dale to keep me company all the way.

I wasn't at all ready for the emotional send-off. It seemed the entire St. Luke's staff from the intensive care ward gathered around for a farewell that will be etched in my memory forever. Coming out of a famine of human contact, I was moved to tears by their hugs and best wishes and heartfelt blessings, not to mention requests for photos. The cheerful commotion felt like a parade. A friendly entourage escorted me to the elevator while another group met me on my way out of the elevator. I was steered through the corridors to a back entrance where the transporting ambulance waited on standby.

After many more hugs and well-wishes I was settled in, Dale climbed in beside me and the ambulance eased away on a quiet drive to the airport. We had successfully escaped the attention of the media. Dale held my hand and just smiled as I babbled away to the medical attendants who put up with it and were openly compassionate.

Our chartered Lear jet sat on the tarmac, fuelled up and ready for takeoff. I could hardly contain my excitement as we settled into the compact jet while the pilot waited for clearance. Running high on adrenalin, I was a non-stop chatterbox. I told the attendant, "if you want me to shut up, you'll have to give me a needle." He responded, "Don't you worry ma'am. I'm getting one ready right now," as he shot it in my arm!

It was Tuesday, May 10, only five days since my helicopter rescue flight. We lifted off, our course set northwest, for the Penticton airport. My spirit had lifted off too. It's breath-taking to be on your way home so soon after figuring you will never get to see home again. Dale remembers that flight much better than I do as I'm sure I slept most of the way there. He said that what impressed and surprised him most was watching me come through the long ordeal as the same person but much stronger somehow.

Long hours after our departure, at 7:40 p.m., the media received this update from the hospital:

> "Rita Chretien, a patient at St. Luke's Magic Valley Medical Center, has been discharged from this hospital and transported to a British Columbia hospital. As the Chretien family makes the journey home with their mother, the family wishes to extend their sincere appreciation for all the prayers and well wishes the family has received over the past few days. They are grateful for the respect for their privacy during their stay which has allowed their family time to celebrate and reconnect."

Chapter Fourteen

Home Sweet Home

When I landed back in Penticton, there was a friendly welcome of RCMP members, fireman and the ambulance team at the airport waiting for the arrival of this Lear jet with a fragile patient from Idaho. What a joy for me to see familiar faces from my hometown and to hear their warm greetings and "Welcome home, Mrs. Chretien!" They escorted me quietly in an ambulance to the back entrance of the hospital to shield me from possible media presence. I sure appreciated that because I was still exhausted and emotional from the whole ordeal! If anyone asked the hospital staff, they were not even allowed to say I was a patient unless they had a password.

I was deposited in the cold, barebones room at the end of the maternity ward for privacy and left alone for what was probably just a short while but minutes felt like ages. My pent-up feelings began to pour out in quiet sobs and tears that I could not stop. A nurse finally showed up to check on their newly-admitted mystery patient. I was embarrassed to be found crying but the nurse didn't seem to take any notice. Shivering, I asked if I could please have another blanket and pillow. To my surprise, the nurse did not return. I was in a panic and feeling quite abandoned. I just wanted to close my eyes and sleep but I couldn't relax.

Dwight and Rita showed up soon after. They found me in tears, curled up on a hard mattress, shivering on the bed. Rita immediately dispatched Dwight to fetch a down comforter and a soft pillow from their home. Dwight smuggled the items in past security so that first night back in my hometown I slept well, with the comforter wrapped around like a sleeping bag and the pillow tucked under my weary head. I could see there was going to be no pampering here! What joy and tears we shared! Rita brought me fresh coffee and healthy snacks every morning at 7 a.m., so we could spend a little time together before the busy day ahead.

My son Carl, who was not able to visit me in the USA, came to the Penticton hospital soon after I arrived to see with his own eyes that I was going to be okay. We had a warm reunion that evening. He showered me with a bountiful supply of healthy snacks, with specific instructions on what to munch on for the next few days—his typical way of love in action for sure! That's when he was nicknamed Dr. Carl. He faithfully came to see me every day with yet another batch of healthy snacks.

The day after I settled into my Penticton hospital bed, Pastor Neil made his way over to my bedside while others came, one at a time. What a joy to be welcomed home! They had to have a password to get in past the nurses' station to protect me from the media and the possibility of being bombarded with too many people at once. My son Dale, who flew home with me on the Lear jet, stayed for a couple of days to spend some time with me and to escort visitors from the nurse's station to my room. He was both my butler and bodyguard.

The following day after I returned by jet, Raymond, Jennifer, Henry and Betty made the long drive back to Penticton. That evening I had the joy of seeing Raymond and Jennifer's two children, my grandchildren, Anyalee and Deklan, once again. It was very surreal for them after already believing I was in heaven. I had to let them take time to understand and feel comfortable with me. I looked so different now, thin and short hair! My other three grandsons, Dale and Beth's children, were far away in Alberta so I had to wait patiently until another time for us to have a visit. I really needed a gradual return to my new reality. It was bittersweet to return without my husband by my side. I was thrilled to be home but it was a struggle to accept that I would never see him again on this side of heaven.

MOTHER'S DAY MIRACLE

On May 11, 2011, my friend Rita sent out another email:

"Hi everyone,

Just time for a quick note; as you all have already been aware of, my "bestest" friend, Rita Chretien is back in Penticton at our local hospital. Last night Dwight and I got to see her and what a sight. She is beautiful. We had lots of hugs, laughter and tears. She is very weak and fragile but with her inner strength, I'm sure she will recover in short order. GOD IS SO VERY GOOD. It has been quite a while since Dwight has seen the spark in my eyes, but now it is there for sure. This morning I took Rita over a coffee and a few other things and had a 5 min visit with her. While there, she had her blood test. Her own Dr. Johnson came to see her and also a specialist on internal medicine. I'm sure she will be kept busy today and in the coming days and I just hope she gets the required rest to heal both her body and her soul. Continue praying for the authorities help in finding Albert and also for Rita's recovery. Once again—GOD IS GOOD.

Love to all,
Rita McGillis"

During my second night in the hospital, I woke up with a lovely sound of Albert laughing and little children giggling with delight! It sounded like it was outdoors and like I was listening from an open window and hearing this, like it used to be when our grand kids were just tiny and grandpa was chasing and playing with them in our back yard. What a joy to hear that! I believe it was a confirmation from God to me, that Albert was in heaven enjoying the company of our own two children that I had lost in miscarriages years ago. Well, it sure made me feel better! I slept like a baby after that for many nights! I sure needed good sleeps to help gain my strength.

While still in the hospital, I found out that my friend and neighbour Anne was in critical condition in palliative care. She was in her last hours of fighting cancer. I made it home in time to visit her just days before she passed away. With permission from hospital staff, my son Dale pushed me over to Anne's room in a wheelchair because I did not have much strength yet. We went from my hospital room, through the basement, and out the back door, crossing over the parking lot with me covered in a blanket and wearing my pj's. We tactically chose this route, all to escape the notice of the media parked nearby as I was not up to dealing with all that attention. It was all worth the effort since we shared some precious moments with Anne and her daughters before she passed away.

My recovery was remarkable and I was able to leave the hospital after four nights with bed rest and many small nutritional meals a day to carefully get used to eating again. My dear friend Rita M. graciously took me in to her home as a patient. She was a very strict nurse! Two o'clock was nap time for everyone in the house. She was already caring for her husband who was fighting cancer. She screened my calls and visits and made sure I got fresh air and light exercise. I sure enjoyed her delicious healthy homemade meals. She was amused as she watched me eat every bite with expression.

My family came to have short visits with me daily at her house where I had a lovely sunny basement suite with a view. Each time my family came, I built up more courage to go home to my house without my dear husband there. I knew they would continue to surround me with their love even as they were then. On their visits with me, they filled me in on what went on at home and in the office while we were missing. With great courage and faith in God, they handled things amazingly well and they willingly helped to make that transition to my new reality a gradual process.

It was good to be back, but it took several weeks of rest to fully realize and sort out my feelings. To reconnect with dear friends and my church family was exciting and deeply emotional! They smothered me with love and attention. I heard many stories of their faithful prayers for us and my family, above and beyond my imagination! I heard more about the media coverage and the interviews with Pastor Neil Allenbrand. The media had come to my church, leaving it to him to respond to their questions. He handled it so well. Neil went through so much, holding up and encouraging my family and my fellow parishioners!

After my return, Neil received many similar questions to: "How on earth had Rita Chretien survived?" His answer to my survival secret often went like this, quoting from Neil's own words: "Rita will tell anyone who wants to know that one thing was needed. That was her relationship with Christ. She looked after her spiritual life. What a great truth for all of us to know when we face the struggles of life." He told the simple truth, that I came through my wilderness experience by focusing on my relationship with Jesus, and all the other things found their proper place. Pastor Neil told them that God was still writing more of my story. "There are so many little miracle stories behind the big miracle. Multiple branches keep growing. Even now, Rita is not aware of them all. In the midst of a story like this there are aspects that are bigger than we know. We're only playing a small part. The Lord chose to push Rita to the forefront. She had the privilege of being an instrument in the hand of God. Everyone who was touched by Al's and Rita's lives had to find a way to deal with and accept the loss, and then deal with the find of Rita, alone. Ultimately, Rita knows that she too will stand before the Lord one day. Al ran on ahead. He took a shortcut and got there first."

Seven years later, I am sad to say that Pastor Neil passed on May 30, 2018. We will all miss him very much. He was a wonderful person and a great man of God, true to his faith and our pastor for over twenty-nine years.

I continued to hear how the whole community was praying, and all over Canada and globally as well. I am sure the Lord heard their sincere prayers. Cards and flowers of encouragement flooded in from people I've never met before, who prayed for us. I received many cards and letters from the USA, some sharing their own stories of hard times. I was blessed with flowers delivered to my door for more than a year later.

My sister Ingrid's husband, Dennis Palmu, wrote kind words from the overflow of his heart: "At times, others including myself have looked back and thought or voiced what we could have or would have done to avoid what happened to Rita and Albert. It is easy to dispense advice from a position of comfort and knowledge after the fact. How many of us, I wonder, have found ourselves in a situation where circumstances coupled with our decisions have conspired to bring us to a place of fear and regret? Regardless of where we want to put blame—because that is our nature—we still have to dig deep within ourselves, to persevere and to recognize God's hand in our lives. Is that not what Rita did? Her survival is a testament to her faith in God and her inner strength of character. It is a lesson to all of us."

Chapter Fifteen

Sweet Memories

In the passing hours of recovery, my mind rehearsed much of my life. My thoughts went back to 1992, to the day we moved to a nice neighborhood near the beautiful sandy beaches of Skaha Lake in Penticton. Our new next-door neighbors watched us unload our moving truck. Anne and Tom hadn't met our family yet but they noted that three teenage boys were part of the package and wasn't that a guarantee for trouble! "Mark my words," Anne warned her husband. "Our neighborhood is ruined! We're going to have to move!" Our boys were normal kids all right, active and rambunctious, but not troublemakers. We hadn't driven them away after all, just the opposite. Tom and our middle son, Dale, hit it off right from the start. Tom was retired and Dale, a grade 9 student, gave him a hand with projects like fence repairing and lawn mowing. Despite the age gap, they shared interests in cribbage and pool and liked hanging out together.

Over time, I struck up a friendship with Anne. She wasn't easy to get to know. She had a nit-picky way of finding fault and that drove most people away. I didn't let her get under my skin. I knew she had a tender spot in her heart for me. We enjoyed many visits over tea and sharing recipes. On good days, we talked of flowers and gardening over the backyard fence. On bad days, I took her down moods in stride. She took subtle jabs at our Christian faith. As I clipped roses along our shared fence, she taunted me. Anne was curious about what made our family tick. She asked in different ways how it was that we all got along and seemed so downright happy. I told her the truth: we had Jesus in our lives and that made all the difference. She always responded, "That Jesus stuff is okay for you but I don't like religion."

After Tom passed away Anne grew more sad and isolated. In the months leading up to our Las Vegas trip, she was not well. While stranded in the wilderness, I wondered how she was. I knew she would be missing me, and I missed her too. Anne had become like a second mother to me. Small things matter! Anne's health concerns spurred her to purchase a giant-sized bottle of Omega-3 fish oil capsules—the good fatty acid. She found them too big to swallow but couldn't return the opened bottle for a refund. Not long before we left for our trip, she gave me the nearly-full bottle. I appreciated the timing because our supply was almost out. It was that mega-sized bottle that I tossed into my ice cream bucket at the last second of packing, a real life saver for me. I am grateful that I could see her before she passed on. I believe she trusted in Jesus before her passing. I will always have a sweet memory of our friendship.

In our tight-knit circle of friends, one couple was extra distraught about our disappearance. Dwight and Rita McGillis had been planning to come along with us to Las Vegas. It would probably have been our last trip together because Dwight was in the final stages of a vicious form of cancer. Only by sheer stubborn force of will was he still alive, five years beyond expectations. In the days leading up to our Nevada trip, Dwight's name came up for a medical treatment in Edmonton, Alberta, so we had to part ways. Al and I turned south toward Nevada as Dwight and Rita set off to the north. We didn't make too much of our goodbye, after all, in ten days or so, we would all be back picking up the good times where we had left off.

I thought about Dwight and Rita and how we became fast friends. There was a time when all of their friends were drinking buddies. Back in that day Dwight described himself as "an angry, heavy-drinking man with rough ways." He owned a construction company so he and Al found themselves working on some of the same sites. It puzzled Dwight that Al and another co-worker never swore. He aimed to find out how they did that. Working on a church building project, he watched and listened until one day he walked in those church doors, determined to find out what the no swearing thing was all about, "This, he said to himself, is where I will find out how to change my ways." He arrived home from work that day to announce to his astonished wife that he was fixing to buy himself a Bible. He wasn't much of a reader but after he bought that first Bible he got into reading and couldn't put it down. He hid himself away and read the whole thing through, keeping a dictionary on hand for words that were new to him. He never put that Bible down. As soon as he finished he started over. When it fell apart he got himself another one. His eyes got so set on reading he couldn't focus any more on a TV screen. The more Dwight read the more clearly he came to see that the difference in people is in how close they get to Jesus. He had always believed in God. He just hadn't known him. He didn't even know that you could know Him. For him, coming close to Jesus was like turning off one switch and turning on another. He became a brand-new man who never swore again and who discovered it was way more fun to not drink.

I met Rita and Dwight for the first time when they visited our church. We thought both our husbands were kidding when they introduced us to each other. They both said, at the same time," This is my wife Rita." I invited them over for Sunday lunch and that was the start of our friendship, over twenty years ago. She became Rita M and I was Rita C. We discovered we're kindred spirits, born in the same year; she in Terrace Bay, Ontario, and me, in Terrace, British Columbia. We both looked after the bookkeeping for our family's business. Our favorite hobby was sewing. It was uncanny that we had the same taste in almost everything.

Our foursome took long road trips together, and short day trips. We spent a full day at the BC Interior Exhibition, the annual Armstrong fall fair in the north Okanagan Valley. Whenever we lost track of Al, we always knew we'd find him cruising the rows of shiny earth-moving machines where he was in his element—just like a kid in a candy shop.

We played cards almost every week, always "Rook." Once when we shared a hotel room to save money there was so little space we set up the ironing board between the two beds as our card table. Al was super competitive but he made every game fun. If his team lost, he'd retally the score until it somehow turned into a win or a draw. If that didn't work out he'd coax us into playing another hand for one more chance at winning. More than once us girls let the guys win just to end the game. Dwight understood Al. He knew it was just his style to do everything, at work and at play, the best he could, never half-heartedly. He tears up when he tells you he couldn't have asked for a better friend.

Chapter Sixteen

Rita's New Normal

Al's brother Henry and his wife Betty were caretaking our home while we were missing. As soon as her teaching job finished on Fridays, Betty would take a Greyhound bus from Burnaby to join Henry at our home in Penticton for weekends. She felt she was too upset and distracted to drive the winding Hope-Princeton highway. Spring arrived and they noticed the bareness in my yard after winter. I usually had many flowers on the patio and a vegetable garden started by the end of April. Betty decided not to put flowers in the planters yet. But as spring went on she told Henry, "I can't do this. We've got to plant the garden and get some flowers!" She asked herself, "How would Rita keep this yard?" She bought flats of flowers and instructed Henry on how and where to transplant them, so it looks like Rita's at home. Tending to the colorful spring flowers was their beautiful way to live by faith and to love my family. They planted all my patio pots with flowers and started the yard clean up.

After three weeks at Rita and Dwight's, I returned to my own home to live there. What a joy to see all my patio planters already planted with beautiful flowers bursting forth with their first blooms. She wanted our yard and patio to look beautiful as always. What a wonderful welcome home! Sitting out on my patio, soaking in the sun and enjoying the lovely flowers helped so much in my recovery and time of mourning.

It was difficult emotionally, but I just needed to be home while the search was still on for Albert. I needed to be there because our excavating and trucking business needed my help. When I came home, I saw that the business was continuing in good order. I was so proud of them all. What faithful friends and family! My son Raymond took over the office duties in our absence and did an excellent job. Henry's presence and help was appreciated by my sons and our employees. He helped with company matters wherever he was needed. Raymond took charge and kept the business going amid all the drama. I knew I could count on him! His wife Jennifer was not only his strong faithful back up encourager but also for the whole family! I'm sure she could write a book on it. Carl carried on operating equipment and helping Raymond manage the daily operations of the business. Our friend Dave Goertzen was a huge help as well, particularly with dispatching and with handling calls from media. It took team work and they did it well! I prayed for them all every day while I was stranded. I needed to stay connected to them. I felt they needed prayer as much as I did.

It was good I returned home to get back to work. Dave needed to be relieved. Raymond was eager to get back to his own Job at the post office as well. Raymond still came in regularly after his day job to help with bookkeeping and coaching me for a couple more years. I was able to transition into a full time role with the office duties and dispatching. Carl continued to work with me in the company and did very well filling in the gap where his father left off. Henry also helped occasionally whenever needed. In years past he had worked with Al on some jobs. He knew the routine. At first I took the business calls and dispatching from my recliner chair with note book in hand as I still needed a lot of rest and healing. The months and years flew by. I kept very busy managing our business and expanding my knowledge and experience in the daily duties of the company.

Soon after I returned to my own home, the Lord reminded me that his spirit was still with me. Every night I was awakened by a noise that sounded like a dinner bell at about 3:00 a.m. At first I wondered if I had a heavenly visitor, but I could see nothing. I got up and thought I should pray for whatever came to mind and then quietly sing myself to sleep. This happened every night for many weeks at the same time. It was comforting and rejuvenating and gradually became a routine, without a bell, during the next several months. I carried on what I did out in the mountains, singing songs and praying out loud to Jesus. I listened for his quiet voice, making sure I kept up my conversations with the Lord every day. I really cannot live at peace without that closeness. Whenever I was overwhelmed with life and all my responsibilities with our business, I would take a little break and spend time to pray a while. Those were precious times! I could face whatever I needed to do that day. My life gradually adjusted to my new normal. Although I expected my spiritual life would be similar to how it was before, I found that my trust in the Lord increased significantly, causing my relationship with Him to become much more intimate.

My grandkids, Anyalee and Deklan, were a big part of my healing and were such good company for me. Coming over and spending time with me after school while I was recovering was good for me and good for them. One day Deklan found the suitcase that contained Al's old clothes. I assured him that Grandpa was in heaven and didn't need his shirts and pants anymore and that I would give them away soon to someone who needs them.

While we were missing, Deklan took some of Grandpa's favorite trucks (office model toys) home to take care of them while Grandpa was away. He also took Grandma's big teddy bear home. When I returned home he brought the teddy bear back to the house and tucked him under the covers on Grandpa's side of the bed so that I wouldn't be lonely. He was truly concerned for me. He missed grandpa and so did I. It did not take a lot of convincing from me that he should keep Grandpa's favorite trucks forever. We found more of Grandpa's model trucks and equipment later, tucked away in boxes. Deklan was proud to help me sort them and to share them with his cousins.

I am the least likely person to be able to manage in solitary confinement. If you had asked me in advance, I would have said that I couldn't have done it. What seemed impossible for forty-nine days became doable by taking things one day at a time, just as I do now.

There are always new challenges that surface. My relationship with Jesus has always been there, but now it's a deeper walk. Without Jesus there's not enough meaning to be excited about life. Each new day is a gift because God is here to guide me. I've learned that the future is not in my control—it belongs to Him. All my senses are tuned differently. Now I see with new eyes.

For a Christmas tea party gathering of ladies in my neighborhood, I was unsure of how I should share my story. They were curious about my wilderness experience of course. I didn't want to sound preachy. To prepare, I casually jotted down an outline of a typical day in my "new normal" life. Without trying too hard (I've never written a poem before) it turned into a freestyle poem, in Dec 2012, which I titled:

A Recipe of Hope

Start my day with Jesus Christ. Prayer and meditation will suffice.
Eat a hearty breakfast, down the hatch. Savor dark roast coffee to relax.
Feeling sorry for myself, OH RATS! What a waste of time is that!
Tell the devil, "Take a hike!" Not going to let him plan my plight.
Think on what is pure and holy. Thankfulness and gratitude only,
Eat three healthy meals a day. Time with friends is A-OK.
Keep working hard at daily chores. Don't let these things become a bore.
Take a walk and breathe fresh air. Notice all the beauty there!
Enjoy my evening tea and read. Correspond with dear friends, indeed!
Living one day at a time, Worry about tomorrow is not mine!

> I know who holds the future and I know the One
> who holds my hand.

As time went on I gained back my physical strength and confidence. Being involved in my church was a joy at the beginning of each week and again in the middle of the week when a small group of friends came to my house for prayer, Bible study and friendship. Because of the big news story and publicity, I was meeting new people every week. I was careful to not overdo it but some was enjoyable.

Friends helped fill the void I felt when I came home to live my life without my husband Albert by my side. They phoned and dropped by for visits and often included me in their social activities. My personal life certainly has been a growing experience with many changes. I have gradually learned to be bolder, overcoming my shyness. People are very interested in hearing details of my "mountain experience." I have had many invitations over dinner with my friends and their friends, to share my testimony. I have shared in group settings several times over the years. It has been a joy to share and a form of therapy as well. I have come to realize many people have a story to tell of their life struggles and their victories through them. There's always somebody dealing with something tough, needing encouragement and the Lord's help.

I continued to hear what people were saying about me. Many emails of encouragement poured in for months. My dear neighbor, Hannah, was a great help and encourager in many ways. She often arranged and screened speaking opportunities to share my story and testimony. Hannah took it upon herself to make sure the search parties continued as long as possible while we were both missing, and also to search for Albert after I was found. She went way above the call of duty and I will always be grateful to her for that.

Chapter Seventeen

Tour of Gratitude

Hannah organized a road trip, "a tour of gratitude," leaving on the Saturday of the third week of September 2012. The five of us—Hannah, her husband Ken, Henry, Betty and I—left with great anticipation. Until then, I never pictured myself setting foot ever again in those mountains. Not in my wildest imagination! My one long stay was quite enough for a lifetime! But a part of my heart stayed in the mountains. I had not forgotten that countless Americans gave their best effort and showed incredible kindness to a lost and found Canadian. Many of our friends and family and even strangers to us went out to volunteer with the search for us. People are kind when there is a tragedy. Many hunters and hikers were still keeping watch for Albert's remains.

As the seasons came and went, the conviction that I had unfinished business to look after in Nevada grew stronger. I told friends and family that I wanted an opportunity to express my personal thanks to some of the key people involved in the search. It was hard to imagine revisiting our stuck place, the site of my long solitary confinement. Later in the autumn, when the ground was dry and firm, and with my tour of gratitude entourage, it felt safe to go back there.

Hannah helped me make a list of places to visit and people to thank. It would be my chance to share my survival story of God's protecting love and grace, to assure these good people that I am well in every way, and to express our family's deep appreciation for their continued search efforts for Al. I hoped to bring blessing and encouragement to those we visited with.

On Saturday, September 15, 2012, a lovely autumn day, we five climbed into my still-trusty Chevy Astro van and embarked on our cross-border road tour. We cruised in to Baker City, Oregon, first to thank the on-the-ground coordinator of the initial search effort, and then planned a public community meeting for on our way back in a few days.

We pressed on to Boise Idaho the next day for the morning service at the Nazarene church. We had a lovely visit over lunch with Bev and Terry Martins, who were on staff there. We carried on to the Twin Falls Nazarene Church that evening for their meeting. Through an interview with Pastor Steve Myers, I shared my wilderness experience, telling them how Christ's sweet presence carried me through to the day of my rescue and how the Lord healed my body, mind and spirit. What a joy it was to meet and spend time with these kind people who had prayed for us to be found.

Then on to St. Luke's the next morning to visit with and thank the nurses and doctors at the hospital whose specialized care brought me back from the brink of death. What an awesome reunion, which was just as I had anticipated!

That afternoon we travelled to Elko City to meet up with my rescuers, Troy Sill and his family, for an evening meal and visit. I was thrilled to see them again. I hadn't seen them since the helicopter lifted off for Twin Falls, the day of the rescue. This was my chance to properly thank them in person. From the first day they made it clear they wanted no special recognition or limelight. A year and a half later, they were still humbly not taking credit for my rescue. We were glad they agreed to take us out on our day trip. Scott C. Hammond, PhD and author of the book "Lessons of the Lost", also graciously joined the excursion. The next morning, with both capable men and their trucks, we went out to my Mud Trap location. It meant a lot to me, with family and friends, to get out there for more closure and to send up a clear prayer for my missing husband once again.

The bumpy switch-back trail ride was every bit as rough as I remembered. It was Henry's third experience driving on the confusing patchwork of forestry service roads, marked with numbers but no names. He and Betty were out there that summer to scout out the area where Al and I were stranded in 2011. A long way in, we reached the terrain that was eerily familiar to me. We parked the trucks by the exact spot near the rutted ditch, still visible against the hillside. There were the boulders Al had placed to stabilize the van. I pointed out the beaten track that led down to the watering hole. We climbed the slopes to gaze out at the many-layered mountain ranges. Over there was the bluebird meadow. There, where the trail turned a corner and disappeared, was the last place I saw Al, where he stood to blow a goodbye kiss. Around the rock-lined, never-used fire pit we held hands in a circle, bowed our heads and thanked our faithful Heavenly Father for his relentless pursuing love and for his kind mercy to me. We asked for his guiding hand to find Albert soon, for complete closure on this mystery of where he had his last breath. While out there at the site, the Sill family presented me with a gift that is priceless to me—the shed elk antler they found on the day they found me. That antler has a high profile place of honour above my fireplace to this day! We left the hills behind, a bittersweet taste lingering for the remainder of our tour.

Our next tour destination was to meet with Sergeant David Prall and his wife in Elko City for coffee—just a casual off duty visit. He enlightened us on the challenges of the search for Albert. I had a lot to share with them too. It was a very nice visit for all of us.

Our next stop was in Mountain City, the place Al set out for but never reached. The tiny north-eastern Nevada town, sitting in the middle of nowhere at an elevation of about six thousand feet, is set in a narrow valley circled by rounded snow-capped mountains. There at Mountain City we were treated to legendary American hospitality. The managers of the Chambers Motel, Shorty and Butch in their own home, prepared a special evening feast for the lost-and-found Canadian lady and her troop of friends. We had a heartwarming visit for sure! We slept soundly in the clean cool mountain air motel rooms. Early the next morning we were invited by Lee Chambers for breakfast at his quaint home on the hill above the motel. Our gracious host, an elderly hunter guide and a seasoned scout, knew the lay of the back country better than anyone in those parts. After treating us to a lavish hearty home-cooked breakfast the mountain man spread out the area map. He raised his arm and pointed to a high mountain peak we could see from his porch off in the far distance. "That's Merritt Mountain," he told us. By Lee's own calculations, knowing where our van was stuck, and hearing that Al was not an experienced tracker, Lee concluded that Al would not have made it to Merritt Mountain because of the harsh conditions. If he had made it to the top, he would have seen Mountain City just downhill from there. He told us that no one went up to search that high altitude mountain because the snow pack was still too deep that season while the search was on. It didn't melt all through that summer. "But that's the way your husband would have tried to come over all right," he speculated. My heart sank! What if he did get that far and died there? Mr. Chambers meant well and I appreciated his report but I couldn't help gazing up at that far-off peak and picturing my dear husband still up there. It seemed like Henry could read my thoughts. We shared glances. I wasn't consoled. I felt sadder than ever. Lee wasn't finished yet. He had more to say, "You shouldn't feel too bad," he told me, "because there is no way a man without extreme training, could have made it all the way in those winter conditions!" "They'll never find him. It's a sure bet the mountain lions found him first." If he noticed the stunned look in my wide eyes, it didn't slow him down any. He carried on describing the huge mountain lions. "Here's a shot of one hanging over the sides of a pickup truck. When they come across prey," he said, "they leave no evidence." I felt faint—it was time to go. I thanked our straight-shooter breakfast host and joined my friends. I had to keep my mind on a picture of Al sheltered and safe on Merritt Mountain, not eaten by a mountain Lion. I left a piece of my heart there in Mountain City. We continued on our journey and Mountain City slipped into a cloud cover. The new posters that we posted while out there stood on guard, "*Still Missing: Albert Chretien, Last seen March 22, 2011.*"

We left the area and stopped in Owyee at the fire hall to chat with the folks there. We knew they had some of their crew searching for Albert also. It was my opportunity to say thank you to them even though some of the key people were not there at the moment. Our next stop that same day was the Boise Nazarene Church again, to speak to them at an evening gathering with many of their congregation. I had a warm reception there to share my story with them and to answer many of their questions.

The next stop on our way home was in Baker City, where I shared my story to an empathetic crowd. I didn't hold back any of the sorry details. I admitted that we got hopelessly lost by making a series of small mistakes. I tallied the "inconsequential" decisions that ultimately led to disaster. The hard part was explaining Al's decision to walk out alone to Mountain City but the best part was making it clear that I had survived because I wasn't really alone. I believed Jesus's presence was close and protected me, from the first day to the forty-ninth day.

The next morning on September 23rd, we started our journey back to Penticton. Arriving back at home on that Sunday afternoon our "Tour of Gratitude" came to an end. I was satisfied with what we had accomplished.

Chapter Eighteen

Closure at Last

Just five days after returning from this road trip, my husband's remains were found by hunters on September 29, 2012. His remains were untouched and his body was still wrapped in his blanket. What a miracle indeed! Our prayers were answered. We had already had his memorial service on the Saturday of the Easter weekend in the spring of 2012. Now we were able to have a proper burial and another intimate time at the grave side with a few dear friends and family to complete our closure.

The amazing detail that still leaves me in awe about the hour in which Al's remains were discovered is a story in itself. I was at a ladies luncheon on the afternoon of September 29, 2012 in a small church in Oliver, British Columbia, crowded with women who were there to hear my story. On the way there I travelled alone in the same van that was my shelter in the wilderness. I had a sweet time all the way there singing my special theme song, "His Eye Is on the Sparrow" and a few other songs to get me in a calm mood and prepare my heart to share with these dear ladies. As I walked in the door I sensed the Lord say in his quiet gentle way, "You sing that song to them today." I'm thinking to myself as I walk through the door, "Rita, you are really imagining things! Just ignore that! You'll make a fool of yourself. You know you've never sung a solo in your life!" So I walked in early so I could meet those in charge. I placed a little brochure on each table with the words of that song because I was going to tell the ladies about my little feathered friend and how that song is special to me. The lady in charge said to me, "You are singing it, aren't you?" "Well, no, I've never sung a solo before," I said defensively. "Nothing to it, she responded. Sit down and let's go through it quickly, we have time." Well, there I was, singing a solo! I don't know how it sounded but it was another step in growing out of my shyness.

The meeting went well and I truly felt blessed as I shared with one of the most intimate groups that I have ever shared my story with. They closed the meeting with a very sincere prayer that Al would be found very soon. I left for home about three forty-five that afternoon with a great sense of peace. I felt so refreshed, like I was on a cloud all the way home. I was very touched by that powerful prayer and by the sincerity of those ladies that afternoon.

The next day after church, I went out for lunch with some good friends. Just after our meal I got the long awaited phone call that I had already given up on. Yes, it was for real! Sergeant David Prall was on the phone with good news. "Are you sitting down?" His words blurred in my head. "Your husband's remains have been found. It looks like he died of natural causes; exposure and exhaustion, probably the first time he stopped to rest. You can be very proud of him. He obviously persevered until he found shelter."

I knew it was another miracle. You think you're ready to hear such a report, but nothing can prepare you for the finality of it all. My first instinct was to curl up and be alone in my sheltered home, but that wasn't going to happen. The news was already being broadcast to the world. Once again, media swarmed in from all corners of the world. Our entire street turned into a traffic jam of vans and trucks and high tech equipment. Sympathetic neighbors and curious onlookers gathered to watch the action, hoping and waiting for a family appearance. I called Henry to come over and answer the calls and the doorbell. I just couldn't handle it. I had a carpenter scheduled to work at my house that day, a good friend, so he had a hard time getting into my driveway. He managed to get in by the back alley and was stopped by reporters there, so no work happened that day—too much excitement! My phone did not stop ringing!

The Penticton RCMP planned a "news conference." At first I did not want to go. Henry and Pastor Allenbrand could attend in my place to present statements and answer questions. The media liaison officer, Dan Moskaluk, persuaded me to reconsider. He helped me understand why it was important for me to be present as I was *the face of the story*. It was the media's job to report on my personal reaction. If I attended and offered comments with them assembled in one place at one time, then pressure would ease off.

Finding Al's remains wasn't just important for our family and friends, but also for our community and people across Canada and the US, and people in countries around the world who had supported and prayed for us from the beginning. They had journeyed with us all the way through to this hard finish line. They were with us in feeling intense emotion. The officer assured me I wouldn't have to make a statement unless I wanted to. The RCMP would take charge of presenting the official details and answering questions about the actual search and recovery.

In retrospect, I'm glad that I agreed to be there. The RCMP protected us from potential media swarms by having us arrive early at the station. We were ushered in to a private room to wait and help each other relax. When it was time, a contingent of officers escorted our walk out to the news conference area.

Henry and Betty Chretien, Pastor Allenbrand, and I took seats in front of a sea of microphones and flashing cameras. I held myself together by fixing my gaze straight ahead as the RCMP officer read the prepared statement that officially confirmed the finding of the remains of Albert Chretien. Henry followed up with a statement that spoke for all of our family: "We had long concluded Albert was in heaven already. We now have more insight into his last day here. We now have comfort and closure to this chapter in our lives. Our understanding is that Albert's remains were found resting under a tree. He had placed his backpack where it could be seen and he laid down under the protection of the tree for a much-needed rest and died peacefully in his sleep. After leaving the van he had walked about 10 miles, climbed 2,300 feet in altitude and in adverse conditions." Pastor Neil Allenbrand then concluded with a few words of thanks and praise to our Lord.

Given permission to go ahead with questions for me, the media asked for the first thought that ran through my head when I heard the news. I answered: "You did good, Al. Thank you for your effort," adding, "I know he did it for me. I am so grateful." When it was all over and we left the police station for home, a deeper healing began for our family. Al's journey was over. He was safe in every sense.

In time, we learned the story behind the finding of Al's body. Our freshly-posted missing person poster caught the eye of a small hunting party. The two men, along with one of their young sons, were surprised that "that Canadian guy" still hadn't been found. They talked it over and decided to go up a certain way and keep an eye out. Back in their home community, their wives had also noticed the "still missing" poster. Imagining what it would be like to have a loved one missing for a year and a half, they prayed that their husbands would be guided to the lost Canadian man.

Late afternoon, on Saturday, September 29, 2012, higher up and farther out than they might normally have ventured, the two men and a boy noticed an odd sighting out in the open, a blue something at the side of the trail. They stopped and picked up a small weather-beaten hiker's pack. Inside they found Al's business card. Almost at once they connected this find with the missing person poster. Stunned to think they had stumbled across the trail of the missing Canadian man, they scanned the rangeland around them. A forest fire had swept through years before and left open space, except for a small grove of 10 to 20 foot tall trees, standing about 200 feet from the trail. They left their ATVs and walked over for a look around. They didn't have to look long. Tucked in a hollow at the base of a tree, visible after the summer snowmelt, a human body was curled into a sleeping position, the head resting on a downed log. The remains were completely undisturbed. The men took off their hats, bowed their heads and offered a prayer for the man in the grove.

Leaving their grim discovery in place, they walked back to their ATVs and drove four hours straight, reaching Elko County by nightfall, to report on their find. First thing the next morning they guided a recovery team back in. Deputies officially identified Canadian Albert Chretien from items in the pockets of his clothing.

The location was on Merritt Mountain, at an elevation of 8,150 feet. (The van elevation was 5,770 feet.) In the cold temperatures, in deep snow, in unknown trackless wilderness, Al had climbed 2,380 feet in elevation. He had walked 10.6 kilometers (6.6 miles) to get almost halfway, within 11.8 kilometers (7.3 miles) of his Mountain City destination. For almost half the distance, he had kept his bearings and had been heading in the right direction. When he couldn't walk any further he chose the ideal place to rest, a grove of trees. Because he was shaded by the trees and the cooler season that past two summers, not enough sun reached it to melt the snow cover over him. The deep snowpack served as a protective shield to preserve his remains.

Al had hoped to use the GPS to hike the winding steep terrain but the battery had most likely worn down. In blizzard conditions and battling snow drifts, he eventually ended up at the summit of the mountain. Had he kept his bearings exactly, he might have made it beyond the trails all the way to the highway. He was found just 2.4 kilometers from the tangle of dirt roads that dot the countryside. Detectives believed he hadn't suffered much at all. He probably just fell asleep on the first night or early the first morning and froze to death in the freezing conditions. Search and rescue experts were astounded that Al's body was found fully intact, not disturbed by natural events or wild animals, after the passage of six seasons. They considered that almost impossible. We had our second miracle. To those who knew the rugged land, it was beyond belief that Al had walked as far and as high as he did. To those who knew Al, they believed he would *give it all he got* because he loved Rita and his family. An Elko County sheriff's deputy applauded his effort publicly saying, "It took a courageous man to make it as far as Mr. Chretien did."

He was found at the same time that I was driving home from my Oliver visit with the ladies group, and only ten days after my friends and I had a very nice off duty visit with David Prall in Elko City. He had told us about their challenges while they had searched for Albert. There was such a short window of time between the late snow melt that summer and the soon to be snowfalls again in the high mountain where he had walked. So it was an answer to prayer for sure! It was nice that David was the one to make the call to me. What a shock it was but I'm so grateful for the closure. The Lord was kind to us.

CHAPTER NINETEEN

Family History

Albert

The family was often asked if he they were related to Jean Chretien, one of Canada's former Prime Ministers. Albert's father's name was also Jean Chretien. We are not aware of a close connection.

Born in France in 1901, the Jean Chrétien who was Al's father was the son of first generation emigrants to Canada. His parents settled at first in the Atlantic province of Nova Scotia where they built up a rum running business during prohibition. When their success attracted attention from the RCMP, the family quickly moved west to Biggar, Saskatchewan. The small town's welcome sign, "New York is Big—But this is Biggar," is its claim to fame. Once more they moved to Canada's far west, British Columbia's Pacific Coast. The city of Terrace turned out to be an asthma-free environment for Jean's father so there they put down roots. With true pioneer spirit, their son Jean took to fur trapping, timber pole cutting, selective horse logging, and any kind of challenging work.

He might have been a bachelor forever if he hadn't agreed to pick up a young lady from the train station as a favour for a friend. That pick-up changed everything. Katherine (Kay) Ede was just nineteen, twenty-six years younger than Jean, when she travelled from

Victoria, BC's capital city on Vancouver Island, to visit her mother in Terrace. The kind mature gentleman who met her at the train left an impression with the way he handled his car breaking down. With no fuss at all, he climbed from behind the wheel, cranked the car to a shuddering start and calmly climbed back in. What Kay didn't know was that breakdowns were everyday occurrences. Jean had rescued that rusty vehicle from a watery grave and restored it to just barely running condition.

After Kay returned to Victoria they kept up a letter-writing friendship that turned into a proposal and a wedding a year later. Kay exchanged her comfortable city life for a twelve-foot-by-sixteen-foot trapper's cabin, more than ten miles from the nearest town. The cabin had no running water, no electricity and no plumbing.

When their first child was on the way, they moved to Terrace. Their home soon filled with joyful noises of children. First born was their daughter Pauline, followed by sons Henry and then Albert. Their fourth child, Raymond, was born with a serious heart condition. On a waitlist for surgery, he held on for eleven months. His death devastated his parents.

Jean and Kay were inconsolable until a gentle carpenter-friend introduced them to Jesus, who carries our sorrows. After they welcomed Jesus into their lives, nothing was ever the same in the Chretien home. By the time their daughters Lorraine and Cecilia and their son Johnny arrived, Jean was approaching his sixties. Kay was fond of telling friends, only half-jokingly, "We would have had more but we ran out of time."

At a Christian youth camp in 1962, Albert decided to follow Jesus. He never looked back. Decades later Henry found out that Albert made the same life-changing decision as he had at that same summer camp. Around the campfire with his friends, Albert adopted as his lifelong theme from the song lyrics: "This world is not my home; I'm just a passin' through." If you ask Henry for memories of growing up with Albert, he will ask a question back: "What makes you think he ever grew up?" He'll explain that Albert took after their mom. She was outgoing and exuberant, "a delightful energy bunny." Just like her, he could hardly say anything without laughing. "The twinkle in his eye was always there. That never changed." He does recall one memory—the day little Albert ran away from home. In full panic mode, their mother ran out to meet their dad's truck when he came home from work. "Albert has run away!" she sounded the alarm. "What are we going to do?" Their father calmly answered, "We'll go ahead and have supper. He'll get hungry or cold soon enough and he'll come home." Of course he did.

Henry had his father's disposition, making it easy for the brothers to work together at the family pole business then, and later with our excavating business in Terrace, and then in Penticton, in busy times. They shared a knack for surveying a site and "getting" what needed to be done. "We understood each other," Henry recalls. "We never did need a whole lot of words." Albert enjoyed his work to the full! Albert's parents passed on their robust work ethic as a legacy to their sons and daughters. Jean impressed upon his children to enjoy their work!

On a wintry evening, tragedy struck their family! Kay and the six Chretien children saw a police car pull up in their yard. A Catholic priest by his side, a police officer had come to deliver tragic news. There had been a serious logging accident. Jean was standing in the line of fire when a winch line snapped a tree. His injuries were fatal. Some of the children overheard the officer's grim report to their mother, who was now a widow. The Bible lesson from a previous Sunday sermon immediately came to their minds. God promises to be "a husband to the widow and a father to the fatherless." Albert was almost fourteen at that time. He and all the Chretien siblings had to grow up fast. Everyone had to pitch in and work hard to support the family.

Rita

My siblings and I are first generation born Canadians. My father, Miroslaw Kumpolt, was born and raised in Poland and my mother, Martha Klann, was born and raised in the USSR, which is now a part of Ukraine. They endured hard times growing up in Europe. They briefly had met each other in Germany, just after World War Two, before separately emigrating to Canada. First my father went to work on a farm in Saskatewan and later my mother to Manitoba to work as a Nanny. They wrote to each other and renewed their friendship in Canada and eventually married and started a family. Their first child was Suzanne in 1952, then Ingrid and less than a year later on New Year's Eve 1954, I was born. I wasn't quite two years old when we moved to Terrace, British Columbia.

In the mid-fifties, the Terrace area offered solid employment opportunities. My father found work, first at an aluminum smelter near Kitimat and later at a lumber mill in Terrace. My parents raised three daughters and my younger brothers, Richard and David, with no supporting family nearby. Those were challenging times. My father worked hard to put food on the table. They always had a lovely vegetable garden. Their example of sincere love and devotion to God and their respect for each other were our best lessons in living God's way. They showed us how to trust in our Heavenly Father and how natural it is to live out this simple faith in everyday life, even in the hard times. We had a good life!

A little history: Terrace earned its name from the surrounding natural terraces formed by glacial sediment deposits. The coastal area is rich in natural resources and is a tourism and service hub for northwestern BC. The Terrace Mutiny of World War II is infamous as the most serious breach of discipline in Canadian military records. In recent history, Terrace received international attention for reports of "sky trumpets"—mysterious whining and grinding noises' coming off nearby hills.

Chapter Twenty

As Long as We Both Shall Live

Al and I were made for each other. We liked each other from the beginning. A whole lot of life happened in the four decades we walked side by side. And we loved each other to the end (thirty eight years). He was known as Albert back in his growing up days. He was a handsome strong seventeen-year-old, full of fun. I loved his smile. Also, on the plus side, he had his driver's license. To a star-struck giggly fourteen year-old he was perfect! Albert and I met at a Christian youth fellowship group the year he was a senior high student.

For almost a year, we were just friends hanging out with our youth group. Albert and his older teen friends chauffeured younger teens to and from youth events. I noticed when Albert altered his course and drove far out of his way to my house first. He ran around the car to open the passenger door for me. Then he backtracked to pick up my girlfriend and ran to open the same door so I had to move over to the middle, closer to him. It was an obvious ploy!

Our first *non date* was on New Year's Eve, 1969. It took some fancy talking to convince my parents that it was not a date with "that Chretien boy" but just another youth function. Of Course, such was not the case—I actually sewed a new dress for the occasion! I was not allowed to date until I was sixteen. We celebrated my fifteenth birthday that evening with our youth group friends who shall never be forgotten. The next special youth event was the Valentine's banquet the next year—another *non-date* that I made a new dress for. I promised Mom we would never be alone for a second! Mom and dad were getting the picture and declared the curfew to be 10:00 p.m. from now on, no matter what! In fact the curfew held until we got married.

Albert graduated from high school in 1970 and then signed up as an auto mechanic apprentice, and he worked part-time with an excavating company. He was never sorry he had the mechanics background, but he really "dug" the backhoe work. He was a natural!

As president of the inter-church youth group, Albert was a born leader but not in a show-off kind of way. I liked that. He undertook that with serious responsibility. With confidence and wisdom beyond his years, he talked with friends who were making risky choices. "Why not set your standards higher than the lowest rung?" he challenged. "That way, even if you drop a notch or two, you'll have less reason to feel sorry or ashamed.

I was impressed with his high moral standards. The more I got to know Albert, the more I liked him. He could get all awkward when he tried to explain his feelings, but for me, that was an endearing quality. He was a truly kind and fine young man who loved God. And for me, that was a good thing. We sure were a strange 1970s couple. We loved to pray, read the Bible together and talk about scriptures that struck a chord. Even some of our Christian friends and family considered us *overboard* but we didn't mind. We were content with sweet goodnight kisses.

Al started talking about our future, hinting at something more than a friendship. I was just sixteen when he came by my school for a noon hour walk on a warm spring day to invite me for a picnic lunch. Sitting on a lovely grassy slope by a stream, I was having fun watching Al skipping rocks over the water. He came over and sat on the grass beside me. "Do you think we should get married?" he asked with that teasing smile that always won me over. I answered in the same playful tone: "Sure, why not?" We sealed our streamside secret engagement with a kiss. He quickly jumped up and skipped rocks again until it was time to walk back to my school. Everything felt different. I was in love and nothing changed my heart from that day forward.

My parents liked Albert all right, but they made sure I finished high school before getting married. I had my eighteenth birthday in December 1972, completed my final semester in January and was married on February 17, 1973. Mine was the third wedding in my family in the span of ten months. Sorry, Mom and Dad! At my grad ceremonies that summer, classmates and teachers were surprised to hear the name, Rita Chretien, called out. Who was Rita Chretien? And who was that young man standing with Rita Kumpolt, beaming with pride?

In Terrace, we settled into our first home and started a family. We named our first-born son Raymond, in memory of Albert's baby brother who died before his first birthday. I ran a small daycare in our home. Albert was like a grown-up kid who never grew tired of playing in the dirt. From the time he picked up his first bucket and shovel to play in a sandbox, Albert knew what he wanted to be when he grew up. He wanted to be a DIGGER.

In 1977 we started an excavating business, A&V Excavating Ltd, when our second son Dale was less than a year old. Two years later our third son Carl arrived. I continued to operate a small daycare in our home and helped with our excavating business. The happy energy of rambunctious boys was our reality. I seriously wondered if life could get any better than that!

Fourteen years later, Albert thought it could. He was tired of working in the rain and snow. He figured it was time to dry out and so we did! In 1991 we moved, lock stock and barrel, to Penticton—our favorite summer vacation destination in the semi-arid Okanagan Valley in the southern interior of BC. Here a backhoe operator could work the ground to his heart's content, almost year round!

Our new hometown had a unique history. First settled by the Interior Salish aboriginal group, the site was at one time named Phthauntac, meaning the "ideal meeting place." That name was replaced by Penticton, an Okanagan language word meaning "a place where people live year-round" or "a place to stay forever." Penticton is blessed with long hot summers and short mild winters and also known for its abundance in fruit production. In Penticton, Albert introduced himself to everyone he met as "Al," and the short form stuck. He made new friends effortlessly. He was so much fun that people of all ages enjoyed him. His unique laugh was contagious. We enjoyed our new circle of friends.

At first, he worked for other companies as an operator. Five years after our big move to the Okanagan, we started our own excavating company once again: "Rital Enterprises Ltd." Our son Carl was his right hand man in operating the equipment. Carl faithfully worked with his dad all those years along with other dedicated employees. His brothers, Raymond and Dale, joined in for a while now and then. Those years were good for the company. My role was to encourage and help behind the scenes wherever needed.

Life was not just about work. Al played as well. It was hilarious to watch him have as much fun as our grandchildren, nieces and nephews. He chased them all around the house, ducking under tables and climbing over furniture with delighted squealing children racing to catch him, and when he tuckered out, he got just as much enjoyment out of settling down and engaging in deep conversations about profound life issues. He knew how to keep a fine balance between light-hearted fun and deep authentic friendship. He was not much of a hugger with friends. His trademark sign of friendship was a well-timed, well-placed elbow nudge or a stomp on your toe for some. He elbowed his way into the hearts of friends, young and old, never discriminating.

I meandered through many fond memories of Al that I collected over the years. In any setting, I was never completely comfortable unless Al was with me. I can't have him with me right now but nothing stops me from feeling close when I call up memories of him. Small things mattered to him. I recall when a friend didn't seat us beside each other at the table at a dinner party. After the meal, Al took her aside. "You know," he sweetly said to her, "I really like to sit with Rita at the table." He did not like change or to leave his comfort zone!

Most of the time, it was easy to be married to Al. I understood his love language. It wasn't surprise gifts or bouquets of flowers, which in his view were a waste and destined to wilt and die. His profoundly convincing way to communicate his love was with few words. He told me every day that he loved me. On the rarest of mornings, if he suddenly had to rush out the door for work and forgot, I simply waited. I knew I'd hear from him. If he was already in his truck or pulling out of the driveway, he'd back in again. He always backed his truck in as it made for a quicker getaway. He'd run to the door and call in, "Love you, Rita." On a super-distracted morning, if he was well on his way before remembering, he'd call from his cell phone. His "Love you, Rita" was a gift that never wilted.

Together we counted on God's boundless love, drawn fresh every day from the Bible, our living water. Al's favorite Bible, a King James Version presented to him on November 3, 1970, never got dusty. Taped up and worn, picked up daily by his calloused hands, the Bible guided his steps until the day he left it behind in the van with me. Al's worn leather-covered Bible is a family treasure now. Paging through it one day when I missed Al's presence, I found several bookmarks, older crisp Canadian bills, placed in various chapters in Proverbs, obviously his favorites. Others were highlighted. *"Let him ask in faith, nothing wavering. For he who wavers is like a wave of the sea driven with the wind and tossed." (James 1:6)* and *"Let us hold fast the profession of our faith without wavering; [for he is faithful that promised;]" (Hebrews 10:23)*

Al was clear about what he liked. It was easy to fix him a lunch. He carried the same lunch to work every day of our 38 years together. His old metal lunch box always contained a peanut butter and raspberry jam sandwich. The sandwich gold standard called for real butter and old fashioned peanut butter with homemade raspberry freezer jam. Any change and he was sure to comment, "I guess we're out of peanut butter." In Penticton's sweltering hot summers, outdoor workers keep their lunches with an ice pack, but not Al, because hot peanut butter sandwiches tasted even better. If he could be home for lunch on a workday he treated himself to a fresh toasted peanut butter and jam sandwich.

Daily routines worked for our family. We had our stress-free daily start-up routine down pat. Al and I carried my family's break-of-day tradition to our home. First thing each morning, Al and I fed our body, soul and spirit. We sat at our kitchen table with our coffees, our Bible and our daily devotional reading, prayed for the people and situations we expected to encounter and then we had breakfast.

On Monday mornings, breakfast was a bowl of cold cereal. On Tuesdays, toast and jam. On Wednesdays, oatmeal porridge mixed with loads of raisins, which Al called bugs. He didn't actually like oatmeal. He tolerated it along with the raisins. Thursday breakfasts were French pancakes, his absolute favorite. It was sheer delight to watch him savour the pancakes. Since the Nevada experience, I've stopped making French pancakes. The tradition didn't feel right without him. I couldn't keep it going. Fridays were a repeat—a bowl of cold cereal. Saturdays were waffle mornings unless we had company. Those Saturdays called for an encore of French pancakes. On Sunday mornings, our pace slowed down. Al grabbed a hand full of nachos or crackers from the pantry and sat down by the fireplace with his Bible. That gave me time to get ready for church and often prepared a lunch for after—church company or just for ourselves.

Our home most often resembled Grand Central Station. Right from the start of our marriage, our doors were open. Al worked steady all week, but we protected Saturday evenings and we kept Sundays as a day of rest from work. When our boys were young, Friday night was family night. Saturdays were for card games and oversized meals with our friends and their kids. Singles, couples and families joined us many Sundays for lunch after church. Meals were usually nothing fancy, often just a plate of nachos or roast beef dinner with pie for dessert. Everything about our Sunday was special; the unrushed start, the refreshing soul-filling worship, the good company of long-time and newfound friends gathered around our table and Al in his element, with eyes sparkling. I will not forget those Sundays.

Chapter Twenty-One

Life with Albert

In my seclusion, I had endless time to treasure memories of my dear husband. I recalled our happiest times which all seemed to center on providing for our family. I thought a lot about the great dad, unique in his own way, that Raymond, Dale and Carl had. Al worked long hours so I could work from home.

He was proud of the boys. Dale recalls that his dad was the kind of guy who spent all his time with people. We heard all the time, 'Who are we going to invite over this weekend?' Our friends weren't just our age. Our parents' friends have always been our friends." Carl's interest in earth-moving work mirrored his dad's. Father and son also shared the same sense of humour. "My dad was so mean," Carl will tell you with tongue in cheek, "he didn't let me operate a backhoe until I turned nine. I was already ten before he let me plow snow and load dump trucks. Finally, he let me run the loader when we dug up the whole length of our driveway." I remember that project well. Carl went to sleep every night with a smile on his face. Carl has an even fonder Terrace memory. He recalls, "When I was in kindergarten, Dad built me my own little workshop. When we sold our house, I didn't want to leave that workshop behind so dad moved the workshop down to our new house just a few blocks away." He built that workshop for Carl with three strings attached. The deal was that Carl had to agree to go to kindergarten (he did not want to go to school) and he had to learn to ride his bike and tie his shoes. That was the carrot he needed. They both kept their part of the bargain. Raymond and his dad did not have many common interests. They did not agree on everything and they often had different views on things but both respected each other for theirs. They worked well together when they had opportunity to. He admired Raymond's mature and wise character. Al wished all his sons would work with him full time someday. Eventually, time ran out and they no longer had that option. It was never Al's style to put deep feelings into words but it was obvious to me that he loved our sons. We both did the best we knew how to keep a peaceful home environment, with a high energy father and sons.

Al and I settled minor disagreements and arguments at the end of each day. They're a lot easier to settle when there's mutual respect. My husband was known as a hardworking man and fair in his business practices. I respected his good character and integrity. Giving his best and expecting the best of others, was simply who he was. We had a good life together. Al and I had hopeful plans to wind down a little in the year ahead, with a gradual retirement as our goal. I always prayed that Al would live a long, healthy life so we could enjoy retirement together.

Al did not always keep me in the loop about hazards and dangers on work sites because he didn't want me to worry. Most company incident reports I heard about came from his employees and co-workers who thought I should know, for Al's sake.

One time I learned from his good friend Vic, who worked with him occasionally, about the day the ground gave way under Al's backhoe. The heavy machine overturned and tumbled down a steep embankment into a shallow creek with Al hanging on. Expecting the worst, Vic ran down to the crash site to find him standing outside the machine already, only slightly ruffled, with a plan already formed to get the backhoe upright and then get on with the job like nothing happened.

Here is another story told to me from his friend Vic. He watched as the loader, operated by Al, careened like a giant bobsled down a long steep ice-covered road. At the bottom Al climbed off and simply said, "We made it!" Vic asked Al if he was scared! He said, "Yeah,

I was scared. But we had to get it down!" He usually dodged injuries but not always. The injuries he couldn't hide, he would carefully downplay.

One day he got his hand caught in the truck tailgate. I knew it was bad because he walked in the house and slumped down in a chair. I stared at the blood-soaked old rag covering his hand with work glove still on. I gasped! He sighed, "Yeah, I know. I put my fingers where I shouldn't!" He wouldn't go to the doctor. I had to bandage him up! Then he immediately headed out the door because he was almost late for his appointment with our naturopathic doctor. I could not stop him. I wanted to drive him in case he might get faint! So I got on the phone quickly to her and let her know he was on the way but not to be surprised if he faints when he gets there. Sure enough he got there okay, pale as a ghost! She laid him on a cot and took care of the emergency medical care for his finger first before dealing with what he came for in the first place!

Early one morning in Terrace, Al came home looking like an Egyptian mummy! I gasped at the sight of him—"What on earth!" His entire head wrapped in bandage except one eye, half his nose and his lips showing. "Yeah, I burned my face. The radiator hose blew. No big deal," he explained—I almost fainted! He wasn't home long and off he went back to work in the shop! That was short-lived because he was feeling weak and needed to lay down awhile. There he was again, thinking he was "Superman."

The worst injury happened at our shop in Terrace. When Al was working under the frame of a logging truck, the jack slipped and the partial weight of the axle crashed onto his foot, breaking it. Al narrowly escaped from having his foot cut off. The drive to the hospital was traumatic for his brother Henry, who was working with him that day, but it's almost comical to picture it now. While Henry was driving Al to the hospital, he kept one eye on the road and one eye on his brother who was passing in and out of consciousness. He was thinking that Al was having a heart attack! Henry steered with his left hand and flailed his right arm hard across his brother's chest. He thumped him again and again until Albert roused and shouted, "Why are you hitting me? Stop it!" Henry took that spirited reaction as a good sign. His brother was going to be okay! Henry left Albert at the hospital and drove back to our home to tell me about the accident. He looked very troubled! His face was pale. "What's wrong?" I groaned. He sank into a chair, dropped his head on the table, and told me Al's foot was broken, that he came close to losing his foot and that it could have been even worse. Somewhat relieved, I said "That's all?" I thought for sure he was going to say that his brother was dead!

My high energy husband did not miss a beat. Sporting a clumsy foot cast, he took it easy for a week before announcing that he wasn't going to waste the downtime. He registered for a computer course and lugged his broken foot off to college. Running late for his class, one morning, he smacked his good foot hard on a stair. He had managed to break the toe, next to his big toe or rather, where his big toe used to be. It got cut off by a lawnmower when he was a young boy. This time he warned the doctor, "You can't let me lose this toe too! I still need it: I have places to go and things to do!"

For all his apparent fearlessness, Al fainted at the sight of blood (other people's, not so much his own). That was one reason he stayed clear of hospitals. He made no secret of his dislike for all medical environments. A hospital was the very last place he wanted to be in when he died. Countless times he told us he couldn't think of anything worse than "having tubes stuck all over the place." He wasn't afraid of death. When we heard of someone dying peacefully in their sleep, his reaction was predictable: "Now isn't that the way to go! That's exactly how I want to die—in my sleep!" For good measure he often added, "When my time comes I don't want a funeral. I want a party!"

Chapter Twenty-Two

Albert's Memorial

We had the Memorial Service on the Easter weekend of 2012. We were blessed by many friends and family who came from far away and by many people from our community who came to share in the celebration of Al's life. He was loved by many! We honoured the life of a man who loved God and loved people. Family members, friends, local dignitaries and media representatives were joined by caring citizens who knew our story. We filled the five-hundred-seat sanctuary of Penticton's largest church, Bethel Pentecostal, and many more packed an overflow area to watch by live-stream.

For Al, I found courage to walk down the aisle and take my place with our three sons, our two daughters-in-law and our five grandchildren. Surrounded by many relatives and friends, we faced Al's last photo. His *ready for heaven* face beamed back at us. On a small display table the tools of Al's lifelong work were arranged around his picture. His steel coffee mug, his metal lunch kit, his well-worn work gloves and his Rital company cap were all empty and laid down because his work was finished.

In one hour, Al's fifty-nine-year journey was held up high for light to shine through. Speaking first for the Chretien family, Henry described his brother well. "He was an adventurous man of integrity, generous in both spirit and action, always ready and willing to give to the needs of his family, his employees, his community and his world."

While all that was true, he added lightheartedly, "it was also true that Al was an incurable creature of habit. He wanted only peanut butter and raspberry jam sandwiches in his lunch box. No other sandwich would do." Henry continued, "no one in Al's growing up family was surprised that he chose to make his living in the excavating industry. From the time he was a young boy in Terrace he found hidden joy in digging and moving earth. Al built his personal and spiritual life on bedrock, an unwavering faith. He gave the first part of each day to reading the Bible and praying together with Rita." Henry continued, "Albert was known as a prankster with a zany sense of humor. He had earned a reputation for a highly-principled personal code of conduct, marked by a never-give-up tenacity. When I went to see where Al got stuck last year, to see where the van was stuck and found out he had only a small shovel, I surmised it was that tenacity that gave him the energy and determination to get unstuck. He got unstuck just to get stuck again. This time it was impossible. He couldn't do it. So before he left to go find help, he spent time lifting the van and putting large boulders under it so Rita would have a comfortable place to stay. Tenacity driven by love for Rita accomplished that. Al faced each day with the awareness that life is temporary, that this world was not his home. Nothing summed up what he believed and what he lived out better than the lyrics to his life song."

> "This world is not my home, I'm just passing through
> My treasures are laid up somewhere beyond the blue
> The angels beckon me from Heaven's open door
> And I can't feel at home in this world anymore.
>
> O Lord, you know I have no friend like you.
> If Heaven's not my home, then Lord what will I do?
> The angels beckon me from Heaven's open door
> And I can't feel at home in this world anymore."
>
> (Lyrics and music: Albert E. Brumley)

Because his brother wanted a party, not a funeral when he died, Henry rallied the crowd to give three rousing party cheers of "Yee Ha, Praise God!" How Al would have loved that! In a more subdued moment, Al's sisters touchingly described how their brother's sense of humour and his faithful walk with Jesus made deep and lasting impacts on their lives. Then it was my turn to step out of my comfort zone, to do a hard thing for the man who did a hard thing for me. I walked up to the church pulpit to face hundreds of kind faces and another long standing ovation.

Rita's Tribute to Al

"Let me tell you about Al, my dearest friend and husband. He was kind and compassionate to many. Al was disciplined in many ways. This was obvious in his routine each day. A typical day was: jump out of bed enthusiastically, sing only in the shower! Then fly down the stairs, often shouting, "Yee Ha!" He would take time to read and pray before breakfast, eat, then grab his coffee and lunch kit with his peanut butter and Raspberry Jam sandwich and an apple, then kiss me goodbye. Then out the door he went (usually on the cell phone already) and down the road to plunge into his busy day. He was in and out of our office throughout the day between jobs, always ready for a fresh coffee for the road. At the end of his day he'd enjoy a quick game of Solitaire and would write in his work diary before supper. A typical evening was often a vigorous game of Rook with friends or an evening of Bible study and prayer. We enjoyed having friends over for dinner. Never a dull moment with Al around! If he couldn't sleep he'd read his Bible for an hour or two or get up and work in the office and listen to Charles Stanley while he worked in the office. I never could understand how he could do two things at once and do it well. He put so much energy into whatever he was doing, whether work or play or study. One thing I always admired about Al from the first time I met him, was his real love for God. He believed that when he put God first in his life, then everything else would fall into place. Al lived this conviction out in all he did. Al loved life! He loved our sons and grandchildren and nieces and nephews. When they were very young he teased them and chased them playfully. They'd often scream and hide as we arrived, anticipating his crazy antics. He had a way of livening up a family gathering, often driving his sisters and our daughters-in-law to exasperation. His strong opinions were not always easy for us to accept. Al rarely missed a day without saying to me, "I love you." I have many good memories to cherish for the rest of my life. We were married for thirty-eight years. He truly was a gift from God to me. I miss him very much. Someday, I will see him again in heaven. I appreciate you all coming today to remember Al for who he was and to celebrate his life with us."

Raymond then took the podium. "We are all used to seeing tragedies in the media affecting people we don't know," he said. "Of course, it is entirely different when something of this magnitude happens to you. Through all the ups and downs of this past year our family got to live out what exactly happens when it is no longer just a story on TV." He counted the hidden blessings. "We got to see how our Penticton community pulled together during a crisis. We got to witness the effects of the worldwide Christian community lifting us up in prayer. We were blessed with seeing people on both sides of the border, many of whom we have never met, take time off work to search for my parents. I thank the RCMP and the American authorities and search and rescue groups. There were so many acts of kindness that saying thank-you seems inadequate. We are and have been truly blessed by you."

Surrounded by my sons, daughters-in-law, and grandchildren, I couldn't help smiling as we sang one of Al's favorite hymns, "*What a Friend We Have in Jesus,*" followed by a slideshow of images of Al's high-spirited life. It cheered my heart to see the family photos and to reminisce such precious memories with my family and friends.

Then Pastor Neil Allenbrand spoke his sermon well, with a message for us all. He drew a universal lesson from Al's life. "Al lived every moment to the fullest with the intention that the best is yet to come. We should dare to live this way."

At open mic time a newcomer to Penticton described how her life was impacted by our family's story. "I never knew Al or the family," she said. "I am just someone who watched the newspaper coverage. My mom and I decided after seeing your story that we would never go on another road trip without a Rita Box. In our Rita Box we will put all the things we wish you could have had to get you through those days you were so brave and so strong." She explained she was in training for our city's annual Ironman long distance triathlon, and in thinking ahead to the tough challenge, she said, "When I have trouble going over Richter Pass and pushing my bike up over Yellow Lake, I will think of the strength that Al had to get out and do what he did. When I slink down here at 11:00 p.m. on that last Sunday in August, I will pass this church and I will say I am being strong because he is pushing me forward. I will carry Al's strength in my heart."

Many more people shared about Al that afternoon. As the intensely emotional event drew to a close a number of people approached me to say that they hoped my husband's remains would be found soon. I agreed that everyone needs closure, but responded, "We'll have to be patient." Media representatives with cameras and microphones waited in the church foyer to get a statement from me. I told them, "This was partly closure for us, but it was also to celebrate his life because we all loved him so much." Deeply comforted by the strong show of community support, I felt a weight was lifted off my shoulders. Al got the party he wanted.

CHAPTER TWENTY-THREE

Life after Death

I gradually settled into living a regular routine working the business and now feeling quite comfortable and healthy in my new reality. Friends would ask me if I would ever remarry. I thought perhaps, but not necessarily. I had a picture in my mind's eye of a bookcase with many beautifully wrapped gifts spread out on it in a lovely arrangement. After pondering on this a while I came to believe that these gifts were from God and that I could open them one at a time as I felt ready for another adventure or step of faith. I would say, "Yes, let's see what you have for me next Lord." One at a time I took on new tasks and new roles, all in faith that God would help me each time to do my best. Each one was a gift and a joy to experience.

Four years after my "Wilderness Experience," I found myself thinking sweet thoughts about a certain gentleman who attended my church. I was praying a lot for Dale Harter because his dear wife Jean of forty-five years had passed away after a long struggle with cancer. I could identify with his grief and loss and the struggle he must have been going through. As months went by, my concern for him grew to be an attraction.

He was known as the "Keremeos Cowboy," now retired from his ranching days. Dale is a handsome fellow with many talents including playing his guitar and singing country gospel. I wanted to find a way to get his attention but I certainly would not want to get in his face or make him feel awkward. He is very much a gentleman. So I just kept a close watch whenever I could at church on Sunday or at our study group meetings which he attended now and then. I kept praying for an opportunity to have a conversation with him besides "Hello, how are you?"

We eventually had our first dinner date on the first Friday after the August long weekend in 2015. I soon realized that I had opened another beautiful gift. We were married on November 15, 2015. We had a Cowboy theme for our wedding. That was a special day for our family, friends and church congregation. We had an awesome Covenant Marriage ceremony and message by Pastor Neil during the Sunday morning service, a planned surprise for many of them. They were delighted and very happy for us!

What a wonderful life we are having! Dale is a great blessing to me. Our lifestyles, upbringing and personalities mesh well together. Together we are very involved in church leadership and ministry. Now we are opening these gifts from God together, one at a time. Life is full of mystery, challenges and blessings. Both of us want our lives to bless others. I have retired from the family business and now Dale and I are enjoying retirement together. Our family is bigger now; together we have eleven grandchildren! What a blessing they are! This is not the end of the story but the beginning of a new chapter in my life! God is good! There is "life after death."

Family Photos

RITA HARTER

MOTHER'S DAY MIRACLE

RITA HARTER

Wilderness Photos

RITA HARTER

MOTHER'S DAY MIRACLE

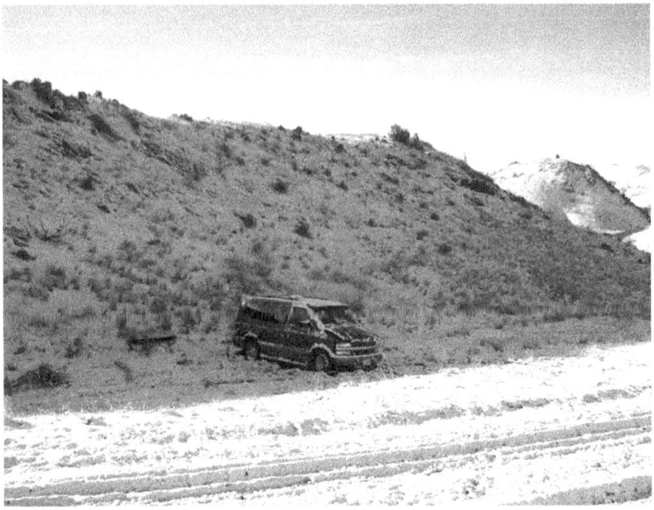

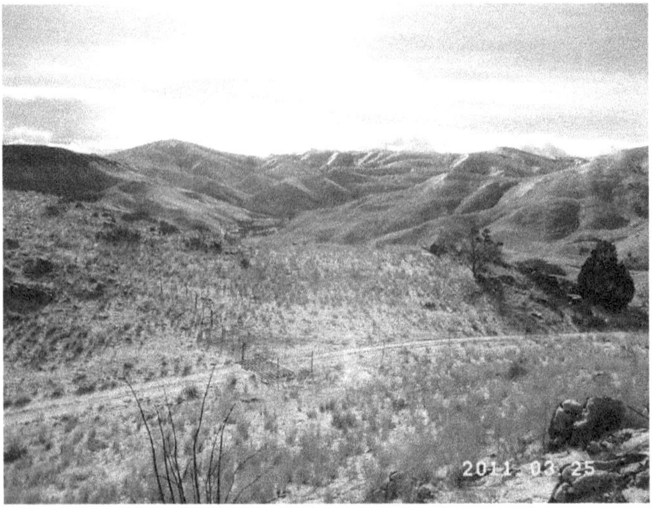
2011 03 25

MOTHER'S DAY MIRACLE

About the Author

Rita Harter is a first time author, writing about her own survival experience, widely known as; "The Rita Chretien Story." Her source of strength is her faith in God. It is not unusual for Rita to face daily challenges that come her way, with hope and courage. Motivated by a grateful heart, she has discovered the key to endurance. Today, she has a new path to explore and new mercies of *God's Grace* to experience.

CPSIA information can be obtained
at www.ICGtesting.com
Printed in the USA
LVHW030250130320
649917LV00003B/4